THE AZTECS

THE AZTECS

Authors Anna Streiffert Limerick, Justine Willis
Expert consultants Joshua Anthony, Raul Macuil Martínez
Illustrators Paula Doherty, Priyal Mote, and Filippo Pietrobon

Senior Editor Georgina Palffy
Project Art Editor Kit Lane
Designer Jim Green
Managing Editor Francesca Baines
Managing Art Editor Philip Letsu
Production Editor Gillian Reid
Production Controller Tony Blain
Jacket Designer Akiko Kato
Picture Researcher Ridhima Sikka

First published in Great Britain in 2026 by
Dorling Kindersley Limited
20 Vauxhall Bridge Road,
London SW1V 2SA

The authorised representative in the EEA is
Dorling Kindersley Verlag GmbH. Arnulfstr. 124,
80636 Munich, Germany

Copyright © 2026 Dorling Kindersley Limited
A Penguin Random House Company
10 9 8 7 6 5 4 3 2 1
001–352669–Mar/2026

All rights reserved.
No part of this publication may be reproduced, stored in or introduced into a retrieval system, or transmitted, in any form, or by any means (electronic, mechanical, photocopying, recording, or otherwise), without the prior written permission of the copyright owner.
DK values and supports copyright. Thank you for respecting intellectual property laws by not reproducing, scanning or distributing any part of this publication by any means without permission. By purchasing an authorised edition, you are supporting writers and artists and enabling DK to continue to publish books that inform and inspire readers.
No part of this publication may be used or reproduced in any manner for the purpose of training artificial intelligence technologies or systems. In accordance with Article 4⓷ of the DSM Directive 2019/790, DK expressly reserves this work from the text and data mining exception.

A CIP catalogue record for this book
is available from the British Library.
ISBN: 978-0-2417-7227-0

Printed and bound in China

www.dk.com

This book was made with Forest Stewardship Council™ certified paper – one small step in DK's commitment to a sustainable future. Learn more at www.dk.com/uk/information/sustainability

CONTENTS

Introducing the Aztecs

8 Who were the Aztecs?
10 A mighty empire
12 Long migration

The rise of Mesoamerica

16 Who lived in Mesoamerica?
18 Ancient Olmecs
20 Teotihuacan
22 Grand city
24 Magnificent Maya
26 Rival neighbours
28 The rise of the Aztecs

The world of the gods

32 It all begins
34 The Fifth Sun
36 The Sun stone

38 A god for everything
40 Sacred serpents
42 Meet the gods
44 Meet more gods
46 The ritual calendar
48 Fire gods
50 The solar calendar
52 Festivals
54 New Fire ceremony
56 Ritual sacrifice
58 Mysterious masks

86 Warfare and weapons
88 Priests
90 Merchants and artisans

The city on the lake

94 Tenochtitlan
96 Sacred centre
98 The Great Temple
100 Coronation ceremony
102 Island city
104 Life on the lake
106 Market day
108 Trade and tribute

122 Clean living
124 Dress like an Aztec
126 Dressing up
128 Aztec hairdos
130 Precious plumage
132 Polished treasures
134 Gift of the gods
136 Writing in pictures
138 Book of the days
140 The art of song
142 The ballgame

End of an empire

Aztec society

62 Who's who
64 The great speaker
66 Supreme rulers
68 Nobles and commoners
70 Lords of the dance
72 Childhood
74 A boy's path
76 Growing pains
78 Spinners and weavers
80 Warriors
82 Warrior ranks
84 Warrior leaders

Daily life

112 Farming on the lake
114 Top of the crops
116 Kernels of life
118 Favourite flavours
120 Healing and herbs

146 Arrival of the Spanish
148 Defence and defeat
150 Surviving colonization
152 Rediscovering the Aztecs
154 Glossary
158 Index
160 Acknowledgements

Introducing the Aztecs

Who were the Aztecs?

The Aztecs were a wandering people who settled in the central area of what is now Mexico in 1325. Over the next two hundred years, they built a mighty empire, emerging as the dominant power in Mesoamerica.

ATLANTIC OCEAN

Yucatán Peninsula

Sierra Madre de Chiapas

KEY
This map shows the scope of the Aztec empire at its greatest extent, as part of the wider cultural and historical region of Mesoamerica. The area comprises what is today central and southern Mexico, Belize, Guatemala, Honduras, El Salvador, Nicaragua, and northern Costa Rica.

- 🟢 Mesoamerica
- 🟠 Extent of the Aztec empire in 1519

The Aztec people
The people known as Aztecs today called themselves "Mexica" (Meh-SHEE-kah). European historians began calling them "Aztecs" based on "Aztlan", the name of the Mexica's mythical homeland. They were one of many Nahua peoples (see below).

The Aztec homeland
Aztec histories tell that their people originally came from Aztlan, to the north, probably in what is now the southwestern United States.

Aztlan is shown here as a "water mountain" glyph, symbolizing a city, its surroundings, rulers, and people.

Columns carved by an earlier Mesomerican people, at Tula.

③ Mesoamerican civilizations
The Aztecs were influenced by the civilizations that developed before them in Mesoamerica, a region stretching from central Mexico to Costa Rica.

The giant stone statues represent warriors.

Building-like symbols represent different Nahua groups.

Each group is identified by a name glyph.

Nahua peoples
Several groups, including the Aztecs, migrated south from Aztlan to central Mexico. They were all ethnic Nahuas (see page 26), and spoke the language Nahuatl (NAH-wat).

These Aztecs are starting their journey south.

A mighty empire

The power and sophistication of the Aztec civilization inspired awe, admiration, and fear in all who encountered it. But in 1519, a new rival, from Spain, brought the empire to a brutal end.

Powerful empire-builders

Aztec rulers were brave warriors and shrewd politicians. They conquered weaker rivals, and forged alliances with others, building a fearsome reputation as they extended their control over a mighty empire.

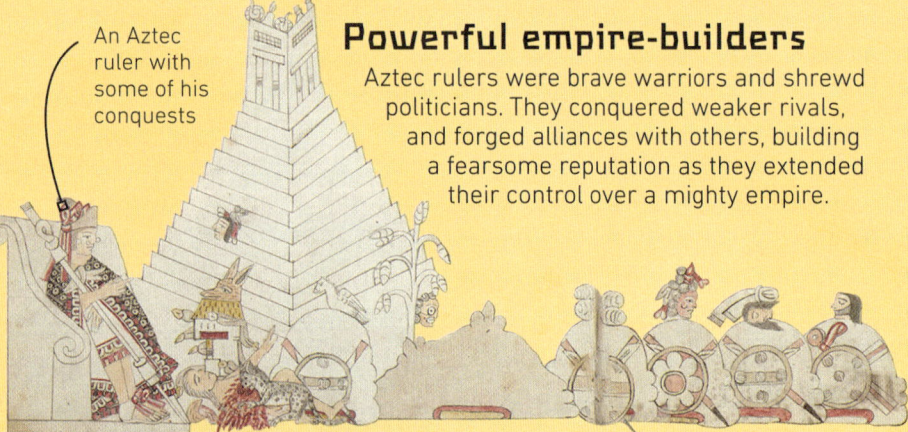

An Aztec ruler with some of his conquests

Gold and turquoise Mixtec brooch in the form of a shield and arrows, symbolizing war and conquest

Life-giving gods

The Aztecs believed life was a gift from the gods, and that they must offer gifts in return. This vase honours the rain god, Tlaloc.

Wealth control

By trading with distant lands and collecting tribute from conquered peoples, among them the Mixtecs, the Aztecs grew wealthy, amassing riches such as turquoise, gold, and cotton.

Tlaloc's face is painted blue, like water.

Empire's end

When Aztec power was at its peak, a Spanish expedition arrived, eager to exploit the land's riches and make this part of the Americas their own. They set out to conquer the Aztec empire.

Founding of Tenochtitlan

At the heart of the Aztec empire was the city of Tenochtitlan. This painting from the Codex Mendoza, a post-colonial Aztec manuscript, depicts the founding of the Aztec capital on a marshy island – the beginning of a spectacular city.

- This building may represent city housing or an early temple.
- Reeds suggest the marshy land on which the city was built.
- Tenochtitlan was founded in the Aztec year 2 House (1325 CE).
- The eagle symbolizes the Sun and the patron god of the Aztecs, Huitzilopochtli.
- One of 10 named men, believed to be the city's founders.
- A skull on a skull rack (*tzompantli*) indicates the practice of ritual sacrifice.
- A speech scroll and reed mat identify a priest called Tenoch as the city's first leader.
- An eagle on a cactus on a rock is the symbol for Tenochtitlan.
- The shield and four arrows link Tenochtitlan with warfare.
- The island was divided into four sections by waterways.
- Aztec warriors are shown as successful conquerors.
- There are 51 blue year signs, showing that Tenoch led his people for 51 years.
- This symbol represents the New Fire ceremony, a major festival celebrated every 52 years.

Long migration

This storytelling map depicts the Aztecs' migration to central Mexico, with pictures of the places they passed. From their homeland, Aztlan (top right), they set off along a winding path. It leads, eventually, to Tenochtitlan, symbolized by a cactus on a rock amid lush marshes (bottom left). This 1704 copy is based on a 16th-century original made by a Nahua community.

The rise of Mesoamerica

Clay figurine with moveable arms and legs, used as puppet or offering

Teotihuacan
At the height of its power a thousand years before the Aztecs, this culture influenced the civilizations that existed alongside it and came after it.

Aztec female warrior with butterfly symbols on her head and chest

Gulf of Mexico

Olmecs
Olmec culture emerged around 1600 BCE and the Olmecs began building great centres on the Gulf Coast in about 1200 BCE. They carved impressive giant heads, and sculptures, such as this seated man.

Facial hair, an unusual feature in Olmec sculpture

A loincloth is the only piece of clothing.

Teotihuacan
Tenochtitlan • Lake Texcoco
AZTECS

OLMECS
• La Venta
• San Lorenzo

Tilantongo • Monte Alban •
ZAPOTECS AND MIXTECS

• Xoconochco

Aztecs
Late arrivals in the region, the Aztecs came to dominate a large part of it in the 15th and early 16th centuries.

Mixtec gold figurine of a warrior-ruler bearing ritual regalia

Zapotecs and Mixtecs
Around 500 BCE, the Zapotecs built a centre at Monte Alban, dominating this region for over a thousand years. From the 10th century CE, the Mixtecs became more dominant. Famous goldsmiths, they paid tribute to the Aztec empire.

Who lived in Mesoamerica?

Hunter-gatherers were established in Mesoamerica 10,000 years ago. The first peoples that settled to farm and later build were the Olmecs. Many others followed – here are just a few of the civilizations that shaped this part of the world.

Maya

From around 1000 BCE, the Maya people began to build a long-lasting civilization. Their city-states dotted the tropical lowlands of the Yucatán Peninsula and the volcanic highlands to the west and south of it.

Royal Maya lady wearing a necklace of spherical beads

KEY
The map shows the domains of the main Mesoamerican civilizations. Today, descendants of some of these peoples still live across the region.

- Olmecs 1600– 300 BCE
- Maya 1000 BCE–1521 CE
- Zapotecs and Mixtecs 500 BCE–1521 CE
- Teotihuacan 100 BCE–650 CE
- Aztecs 1325–1521 CE

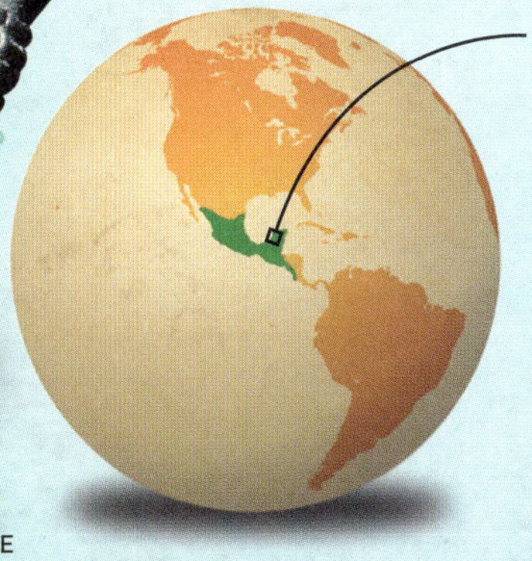

Mesoamerica is the term for a historic and cultural region covering parts of Mexico and Central America, as far south as northern Costa Rica.

ATLANTIC OCEAN
Chichen Itza
Caribbean Sea
MAYA
Tikal
Copan
PACIFIC OCEAN

SCALE 0 125 250 kilometres

Giant heads

The Olmecs left some examples of picture writing, but it has not been decoded and so tells us little about them. However, 17 ancient heads made of basalt rock are thought to depict different rulers. This head is nearly 3 m (9 ft) tall.

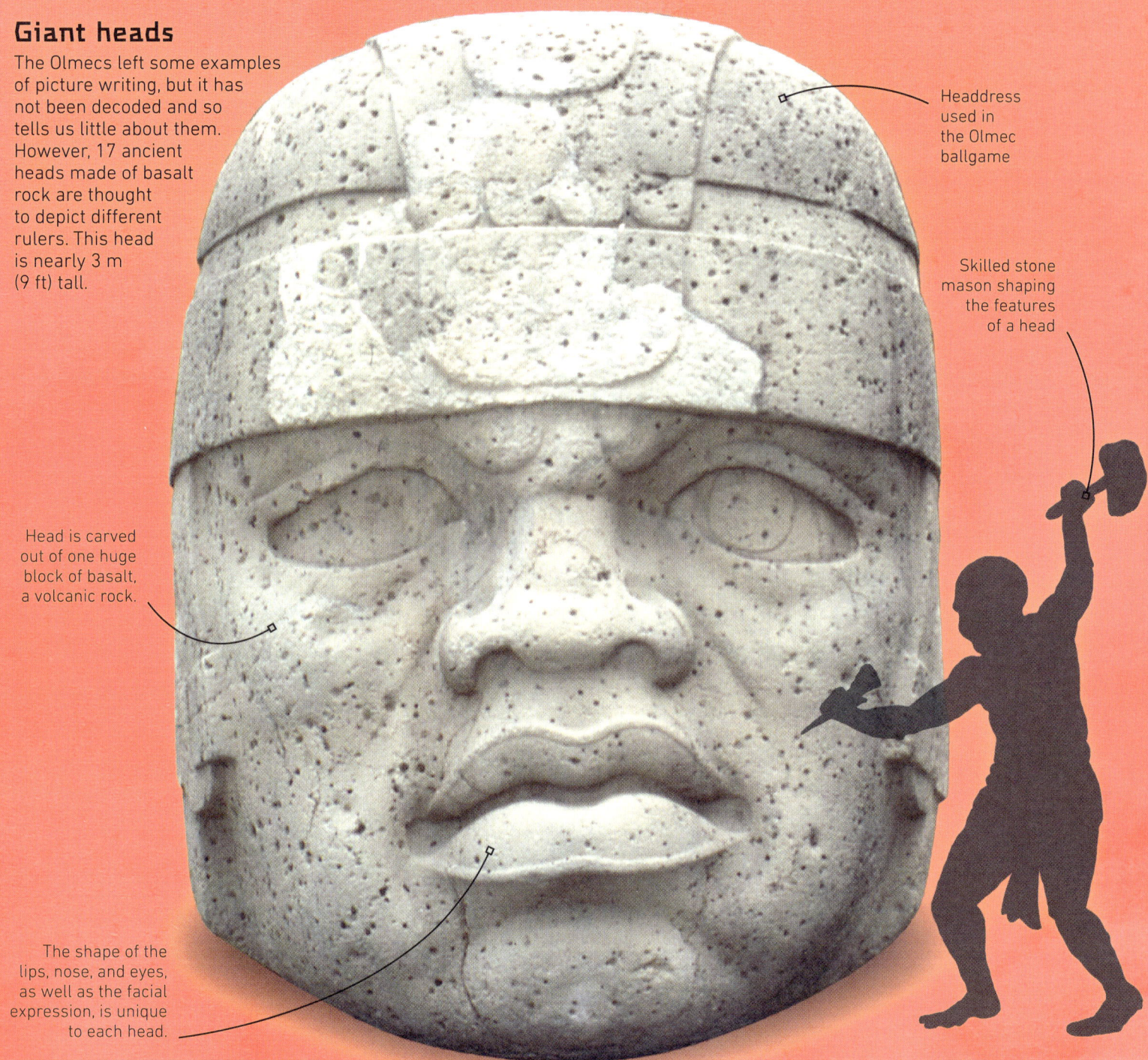

- Headdress used in the Olmec ballgame
- Skilled stone mason shaping the features of a head
- Head is carved out of one huge block of basalt, a volcanic rock.
- The shape of the lips, nose, and eyes, as well as the facial expression, is unique to each head.

Ancient Olmecs

The earliest known civilization in Mesoamerica, the Olmecs first settled in the region around 1600 BCE, developing a complex society. Many parts of their culture – growing maize, the ballgame, their gods – were adopted by the peoples who followed later.

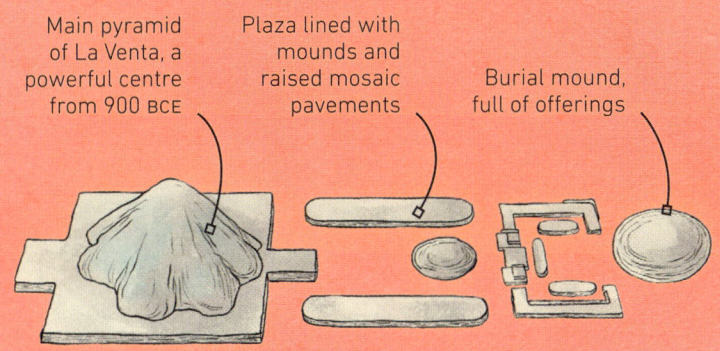

Main pyramid of La Venta, a powerful centre from 900 BCE

Plaza lined with mounds and raised mosaic pavements

Burial mound, full of offerings

Civilized centres

Archaeologists have found remains of large Olmec centres. Their layout, built around large plazas (squares) and pyramids, formed the blueprint for future Mesoamerican town planning.

Rubber production

The Olmecs worked out how to tap milky sap from the rubber tree by scoring the bark, and then turn it into a stretchy substance. They used it to make large rubber balls for the ballgame, and smaller ones for offerings. The name Olmec comes from the word for "rubber people" in Nahuatl, the Aztec language.

Fresh, white sap

Clay baby

Many Olmec sculptures feature chubby babies. Experts are not sure what they represent – royal children, deities, or sacrificial offerings?

Cleft head like a jaguar's skull

Snarling jaguar lip

Ballgame helmet

The tubby baby belly with its belly button looks very realistic.

Were-jaguar

Divine creatures appear as stone carvings and offerings. This axe head represents a were-jaguar, shown mid-transformation from human into jaguar (see page 39). It is made of greenstone, symbolic of life.

Teotihuacan

Built in the Valley of Mexico around 100 BCE, Teotihuacan was the largest city of the ancient Americas. Its centre was mysteriously destroyed by fire in 550 CE and the city's power waned, but it was revered by the Aztecs as the birthplace of the gods.

Mysterious murals

Colourful murals decorated the walls of temples, palaces, and homes in the city. The wall paintings depict people, animals, and religious motifs. This one shows a mountain taking life by consuming people and giving life in the form of water.

- People falling into the mountain
- Butterflies appear in many murals.
- Swirls coming out of people's mouths may represent speech.
- River represents life-giving water.
- Mountain is thought to represent the home of a god.

- Sumptuous palaces, painted with mythical creatures, lined the avenue.
- Avenue of the Dead

Fine features

Teotihuacan craftspeople produced striking masks from obsidian (volcanic glass), turquoise, and other precious materials. They were used in religious ceremonies. The use of masks was adopted by later peoples in the region, including the Aztecs (see pages 58–59).

Distinctive triangular nose between almond-shaped eyes

Pattern made of red shell

Feathered serpent

One pyramid is covered with heads of the sacred feathered serpent, which was first worshipped by the Olmecs and Maya, and later by the Aztecs and their neighbours, too.

The Pyramid of the Moon, was the second-largest temple after the Pyramid of the Sun (see page 23).

The city's grand plaza was surrounded by smaller temples and had a ritual platform in the middle.

Perfect pyramids

The city covered 21 sq km (8 square miles). At its heart was the ceremonial centre. The long Avenue of the Dead was flanked by impressive palaces and pyramid-shaped temples.

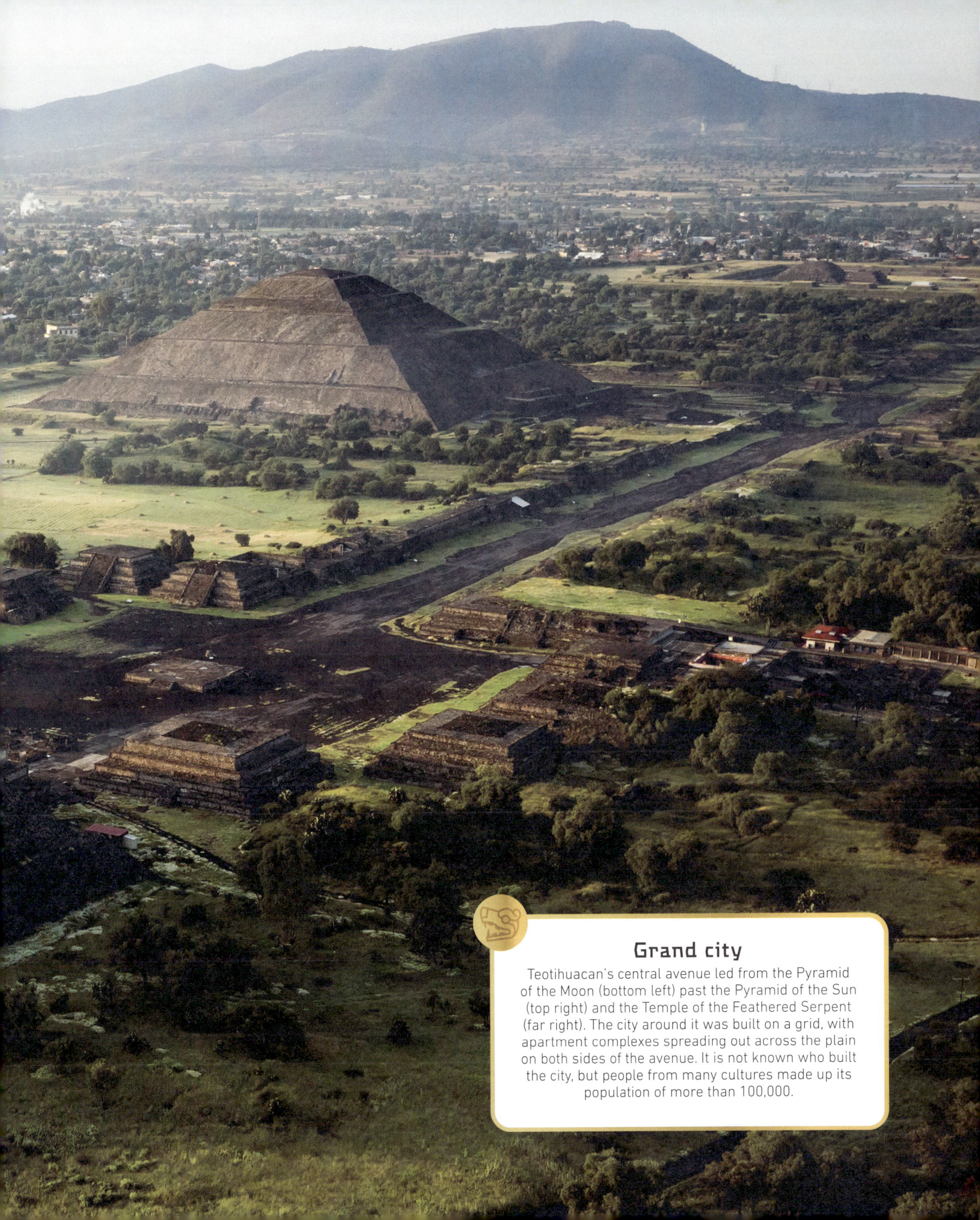

Grand city

Teotihuacan's central avenue led from the Pyramid of the Moon (bottom left) past the Pyramid of the Sun (top right) and the Temple of the Feathered Serpent (far right). The city around it was built on a grid, with apartment complexes spreading out across the plain on both sides of the avenue. It is not known who built the city, but people from many cultures made up its population of more than 100,000.

Magnificent Maya

Maya civilization developed from around 1000 BCE. At its height, between 250 and 900 CE, independent city-states – each ruled by its own royal family – produced outstanding architecture, art, and science. By the time of the Aztecs, the Maya had declined, but remained influential trading partners.

Shield Jaguar II, dressed in quilted cotton armour

Ruling couple
Shield Jaguar II ruled the city-state of Yaxchilan for 60 years in the late 7th century CE. His wife K'ab'al Xook commissioned carvings celebrating his life. This one shows him getting ready for battle.

K'ab'al Xook, helping her husband get ready for war

Jaguar helmet to be worn in battle

Shield

Jaguar

Writing
Maya scribes used a complex writing system to write about important events. It was made up of symbols known as glyphs. Some of these represented a thing or idea, others a sound. This is the name glyph for Shield Jaguar II.

Astronomy
Maya astronomers tracked the movement of the Sun, Moon, and planets with the naked eye or in observatories. They used their observations to create calendars for keeping track of past, present, and future events.

Astronomer looking at stars

- Rubber ball
- Maya players wore extravagant headdresses.

Tropical Tikal
The great Maya city of Tikal reached its peak in the golden age between 250 and 900 CE. Its steep temples rose up in the rainforest of what is now Guatemala. Ruled by a dynasty of kings who warred with other Maya city-states, it traded with the people of Teotihuacan (see pages 20–23).

Playing ball
Like other Mesoamerican peoples, the Maya built impressive ball courts for the ritual ballgame. This stone disc depicts a Maya player hitting a huge rubber ball with his hip.

Glyphs describe who owned the beaker, and what drink it was for.

> The ball was dropped into play. They were equal in strength, but the boys [...] played with all their hearts.
>
> Popol Vuh, a Maya epic story

A servant offers a ruler a jug of spiced, frothy cocoa.

Cocoa culture
Cacao trees grew in abundance in Maya lands. Many city-states became wealthy exporting the precious cacao beans to other peoples, including the Aztecs. The Maya treasured the beans, too, and the cocoa drink made from them. It was served in beautifully decorated beakers such as this one.

Rival neighbours

Long before the Aztecs arrived, the Valley of Mexico was full of different peoples. They traded and fought with each other, every city-state seeking to dominate others, on its own or through alliances.

Seven nations

Many different Nahuatl-speaking peoples settled in the Valley of Mexico. These Nahua peoples all shared the same origin story – the mythical seven-lobed caves of Chicomoztoc, shown in this painting. The Aztecs were the last group to leave the caves, in a faraway place known as Aztlan.

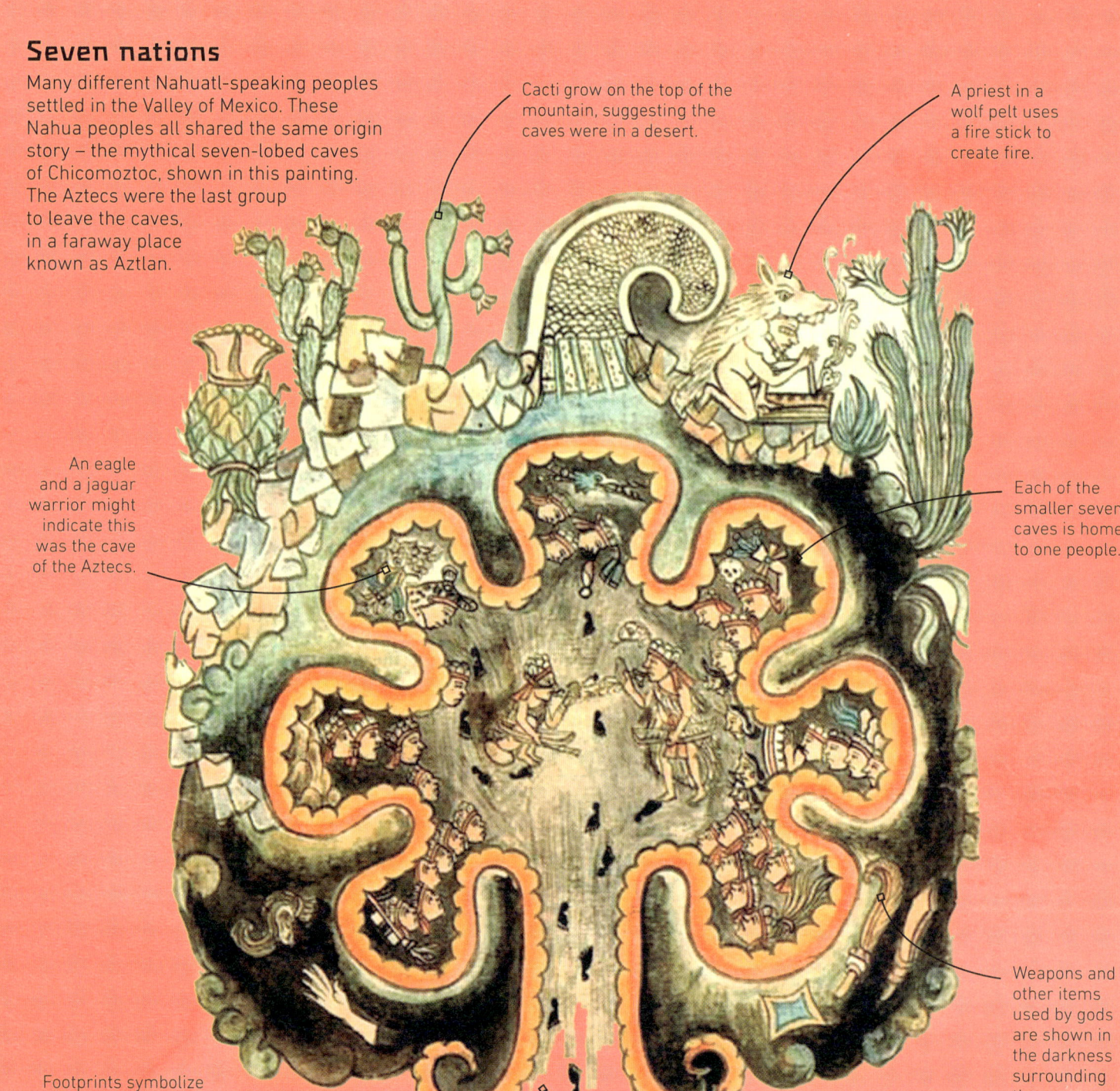

Cacti grow on the top of the mountain, suggesting the caves were in a desert.

A priest in a wolf pelt uses a fire stick to create fire.

An eagle and a jaguar warrior might indicate this was the cave of the Aztecs.

Each of the smaller seven caves is home to one people.

Weapons and other items used by gods are shown in the darkness surrounding the caves.

Footprints symbolize the route in and out of the main cave.

Long migration

At some point in time, the Aztecs set out on an epic journey from the desert region of Aztlan in the north. Lasting hundreds of years, the migration took them to the spot on Lake Texcoco in the Valley of Mexico where they were to build their empire.

Time to leave
After a message from the god Huitzilopochtli, the Aztecs left their mythical homeland.

Priest on his way to hear the god speak

Huitzilopochtli giving the message

On the road
Priests led the Aztec people on a trek marked by strife and combat. They carried many things, including their gods.

Backpack holding Huitzilopochtli

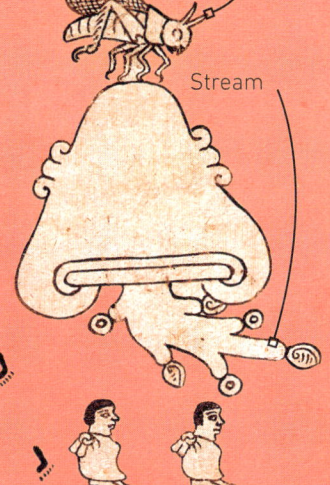

Grasshopper symbolizing Chapultepec ("Grasshopper Hill")

Stream

Temporary home
The travellers stopped at Chapultepec, a hill with a stream. But they were sent on their way by the Tepanecs (see below).

Aztecs camping beside the freshwater stream

Terrific Tepanecs

One Nahua people, the Tepanecs, dominated the region when the Aztecs arrived. They ruled from the city-state of Azcapotzalco, on the western shore of Lake Texcoco. At first, they employed the Aztecs to help them fight other peoples.

Tezozomoc, a Tepanec ruler

Nobles excited at the sight of the eagle

Eagle, a divine messenger, landing on a cactus

Priests discussing the divine message

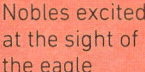

A place of their own

In 1325, the Aztecs, guided by an eagle messenger sent by the god Huitzilopochtli, sighted an island in Lake Texcoco. They settled down on the island, where they began developing their own city-state, Tenochtitlan (see pages 28–29).

The rise of the Aztecs

All of the city-states around Lake Texcoco, where the Aztecs had settled, were rivals. But, in 1428, three of them formed an alliance. The Aztecs came to dominate this Triple Alliance and the region.

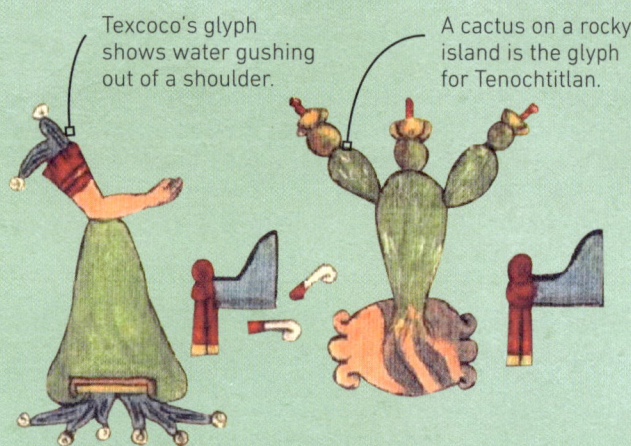

Texcoco's glyph shows water gushing out of a shoulder.

A cactus on a rocky island is the glyph for Tenochtitlan.

Three flowers form the glyph for Tlacopan.

The Triple Alliance
People living in the city-states around the lake resented the power of the Tepanecs at Azcapotzalco (see page 27). The rulers of Texcoco, Tenochtitlan, and Tlacopan decided to work together to defeat them, becoming known as the Triple Alliance.

Glyph for rulership

Texcoco
Founded in the 1100s, this grand city had its own water source.

Tenochtitlan
Since 1325, the Aztec city had grown into a force to be reckoned with.

Tlacopan
A former dependent of Azcapotzalco, Tlacopan rose up against it.

Drum for tapping out orders on the battlefield

Golden conch shell symbol decorates the feathered shield.

Fine feather outfit

Nezahualcoyotl in battle gear. His name means "fasting coyote".

> Even jade is shattered, even gold is crushed, even quetzal plumes are torn... We do not live forever on this Earth, but exist only for an instant!
>
> "Not forever on Earth", Texcoco poem

Wise warrior king
Born in 1402, Texcoco ruler Nezahualcoyotl had an adventurous life. At the age of 15, he went into exile after the Tepanecs killed his father, hiding out in Tenochtitlan. The victory of the Triple Alliance enabled him to take Texcoco back. He ruled for 40 years, gaining fame as a wise warrior who loved poetry, created a code of law, and planned beautiful gardens, baths, and palaces in his city.

SCALE
0 15 miles
0 15 kilometres
Texcoco
Azcapotzalco
Lake Texcoco
Tlacopan
Tenochtitlan
Lake Xochimilco
Lake Chalco

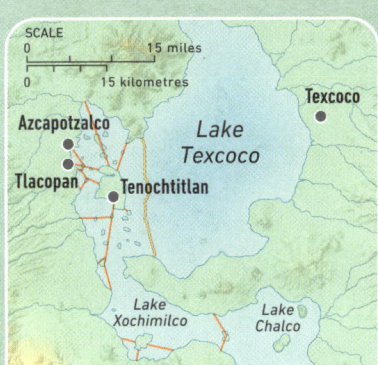

Top towns

This map shows the locations of the three allied cities. While Tlacopan was linked to Tenochtitlan by a causeway, Texcoco lay across the lake, on its eastern shore. The enemy city, Azcapotzalco, was next to Tlacopan.

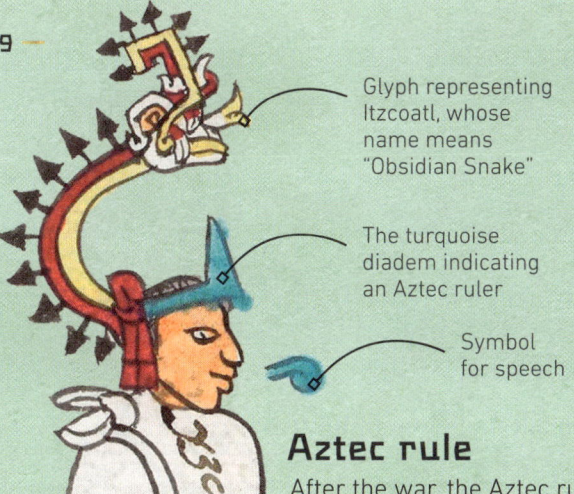

Glyph representing Itzcoatl, whose name means "Obsidian Snake"
The turquoise diadem indicating an Aztec ruler
Symbol for speech

Aztec rule

After the war, the Aztec ruler Itzcoatl (r.1427–1440) made Tenochtitlan the dominant power of the alliance. Soon, the Aztecs controlled large parts of Mesoamerica, demanding tribute from many peoples.

Tepanec war

In 1428, the armies of the Triple Alliance defeated the Tepanecs, ending their enemies' hold over the region. This codex illustration shows fighting inside Azcapotzalco during the final battle.

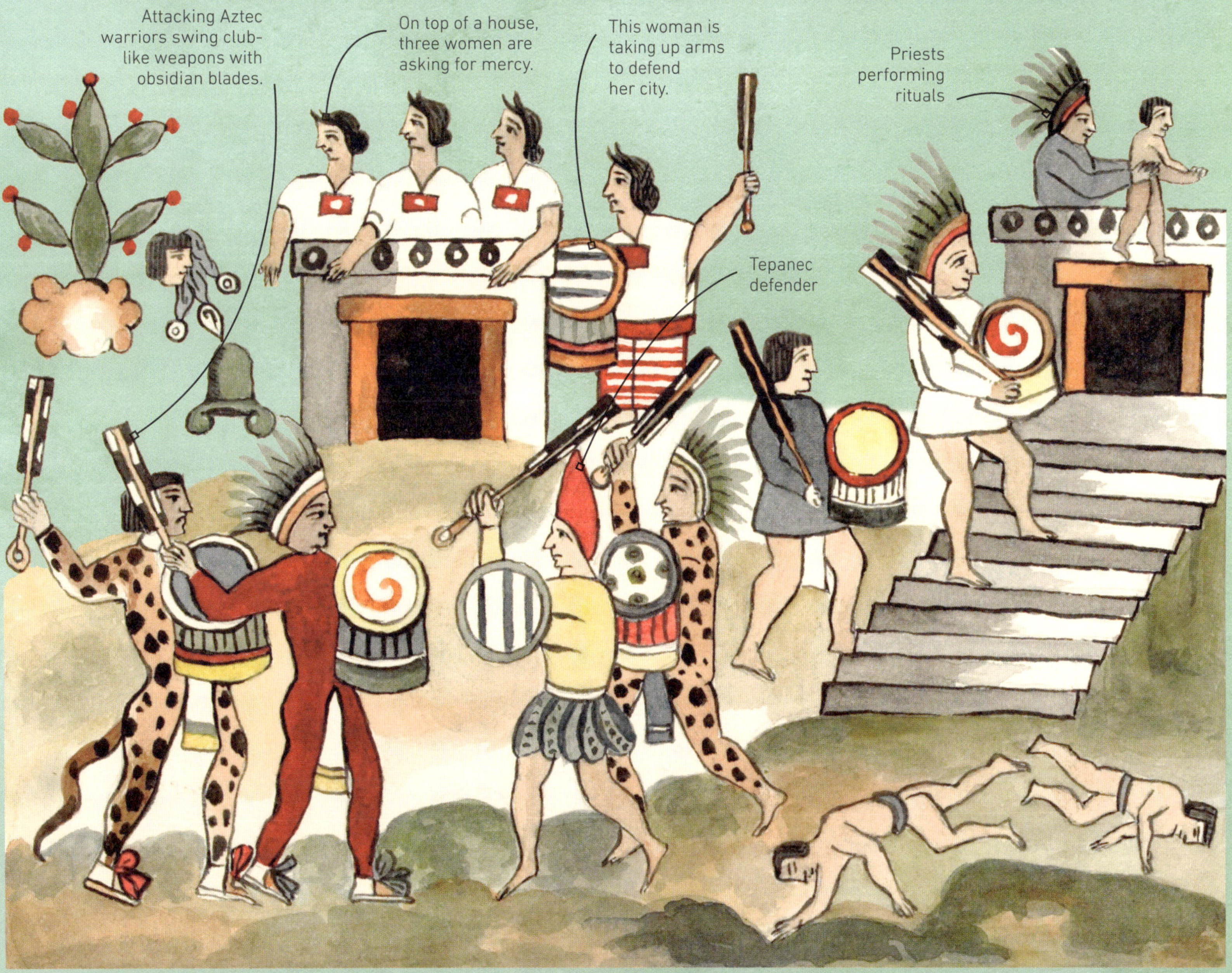
Attacking Aztec warriors swing club-like weapons with obsidian blades.
On top of a house, three women are asking for mercy.
This woman is taking up arms to defend her city.
Priests performing rituals
Tepanec defender

The world of the gods

It all begins

The Aztecs believed that the world had been created and destroyed four times before the present era. It all began when male-female deity Ometeotl gave birth to four sons, each named Tezcatlipoca, who in turn created four Suns, or worlds – as well as other deities, giants, animals, and people.

The first four Suns

The story of how the first four Suns ended has many versions. In this one, arguments between gods brought disaster to the living beings they had created in each world.

First Sun (Jaguar)
Black Tezcatlipoca and Quetzalcoatl both wanted to be the Sun in the sky. Their argument ended when Tezcatlipoca made jaguars eat everything – ending that world.

Second Sun (Wind)
After more fighting between Quetzalcoatl and Tezcatlipoca, people were turned into monkeys. Everything was swept away by a huge whirlwind created by Quetzalcoatl.

Third Sun (Rain)
In this world, Tezcatlipoca stole the god Tlaloc's beloved, Xochiquetzal, the goddess of beauty and love. As revenge, Tlaloc set off a terrifying rain of fire, destroying that world.

Fourth Sun (Water)
Tezcatlipoca was mean to the goddess Chalchiuhtlicue. She couldn't stop crying and so this world was drowned in a huge flood, which washed everything away.

Black face paint

Foot bitten off by the giant crocodile Cipactli (see page 37)

Obsidian mirror breastplate

Tezcatlipoca
Smoking Mirror

- **Compass point:** North
- **Domain:** Omnipresent
- **Superpower:** Shape-shifting into the form of a jaguar
- **Did you know?** The black Tezcatlipoca was Lord of the North. He was powerful and mean, a constant rival of Quetzalcoatl.

Serpent's head and body

Feathered crest

Flint knife

Flayed skin worn as a body suit

Quetzalcoatl
Feathered Serpent

- **Compass point:** West
- **Domain:** Earth and sky, and the morning star, Venus
- **Superpower:** Creator and destroyer who made humans out of old bones
- **Did you know?** The white Tezcatlipoca represents West. He appears in many guises, including the feathered serpent, Quetzalcoatl, and Ehecatl, the wind god.

Xipe Totec
The Flayed One

- **Compass point:** East
- **Domain:** Farming and sacrifice
- **Superpower:** Renewal and rebirth through shedding of skins
- **Did you know?** The red Tezcatlipoca, ruling the East, is god of new life in humans and crops, and a patron of young warriors.

Hummingbird headdress

Weapon in the form of a fire serpent

Shield

Huitzilopochtli
Hummingbird of the South

- **Compass point:** South
- **Domain:** Sun and fire
- **Superpower:** Great warrior who can transform into different birds
- **Did you know?** Lord of the South, the blue Tezcatlipoca is chief protector of the Aztecs and their city. He is god of Sun and war.

Creation gods

The four Tezcatlipoca brothers are very powerful gods. Each represents a colour. Only the black Tezcatlipoca kept his name, while the others are known by the names shown here. Each god is linked with one of the four cardinal directions, which played a key role in Aztec life and beliefs.

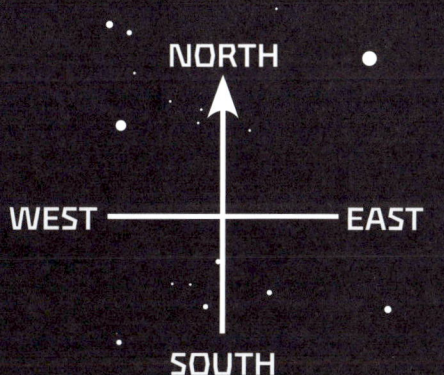

The Fifth Sun

After the world of the Fourth Sun had been destroyed, there was total darkness. The gods agreed that the only way to create a new Sun was for one of them to sacrifice himself by jumping into the sacred fire.

Gods assemble

When all was in darkness, the gods gathered at sacred Teotihuacan and asked, "Who will make a sacrifice to rekindle the Sun?". Tecuhciztecatl ("Conch Shell Lord"), the proud son of Chalchiuhtlicue and Tlaloc, volunteered. The gods accepted and also called on humble Nanahuatzin ("Pimply Faced") to be his second. A huge sacrificial fire was prepared.

Leap of faith

The fire burned for four days. Noble Tecuhciztecatl offered fine incense, while Nanahuatzin could only offer his scabs. At midnight on the fourth day, the gods called on Tecuhciztecatl to jump into the fire. Four times, he took a run-up, but could not bring himself to leap. Nanahuatzin then calmly threw himself into the pyre, burning up and rising as the Sun.

Second jump

When Nanahuatzin rose as the Fifth Sun, dawn lightened the sky. Tecuhciztecatl, seeing the heroism of the lesser god, could not stand the humiliation and jumped into the fire too. Tecuhciztecatl also burned, but he blazed less brightly than the first god. He rose up as a second, less brilliant, Sun.

Tonatiuh, the Fifth Sun
According to some versions of the story, Nanahuatzin was reincarnated as Tonatiuh, god of the Fifth Sun. He reigned over the world that the Aztec people lived in, but they believed that this Sun, too, would come to an end. It was predicted that this would be through a devastating earthquake.

Tonatiuh carries a Sun disc with the Aztec earthquake symbol on his back.

Two Suns
An eagle flew into the fire, scorching its feathers dark, and a jaguar leaped in, singeing its pelt with black spots. Once again, life had followed death, and light had followed darkness. But the light of the rising Suns in the sky was blinding, and it was impossible to look at them. And there were two! The gods could not accept this.

Tecuhciztecatl's Sun is paler.

Nanahuatzin's Sun shines brighter.

Creating the Moon
The gods decided they had to do something. There were too many rabbits in Teotihuacan, and so one of the gods picked up a rabbit and threw it at Tecuhciztecatl's Sun to dim the light. This is how Tecuhciztecatl became the Moon and can only be seen clearly at night. On a bright full Moon, you can actually see this rabbit's outline!

The god Ehecatl throws a rabbit at Tecuhciztecatl's Sun.

Sun and Moon
The Sun remained unmoving in the sky, parching the ground beneath. Finally, the gods realized that they, too, must sacrifice themselves so that human beings may live. They offered themselves up to the god Ehecatl. With the wind that arose as a result of their sacrifice, Ehecatl made the Sun move through the sky, nourishing the Earth rather than scorching it.

The Sun brings light and life to Earth.

Circles of time

The rings on the stone represent Aztec ideas of time. In the centre is Tonatiuh, the Fifth Sun. He is surrounded by the four previous Suns, in a shape that represents the glyph 4 Movement (Olin), his calendar name. The next circle shows the 20 day signs (see page 46).

1 First Sun
A fierce jaguar symbolizes the First Sun, or first age of creation.

2 Second Sun
Wind, shown as the face of Ehecatl, the wind god.

3 Third Sun
Its symbol is rain, as released by Tlaloc, which ended the third age of creation.

4 Fourth Sun
The fourth age, destroyed in a flood, is marked by a sign for water.

5 Sun god
A face, probably of the Sun god, Tonatiuh, represents the fifth, Aztec age.

6 Day signs
The 20 signs run anticlockwise on this ring, starting with Crocodile.

7 House
Not all day signs are animals – the sign for this day is a house.

8 Solar rays
Four "A"-shaped arrows represent the rays of the Sun, Tonatiuh.

9 Claws
Left and right of the Sun god's face, claws clutch human hearts.

10 Fire snakes
Two fire serpents meet face to face. Gods peer out of their jaws.

Fifth Sun
The symbol for the fifth age is 4 Movement (Olin), represented by the shape at the stone's centre.

The Sun stone

A massive, carved slab of volcanic rock that once lay in the Great Temple of Tenochtitlan, the Sun stone is today an icon of Mexico. It is also known as the calendar stone and archaeologists think it was once painted, like this replica.

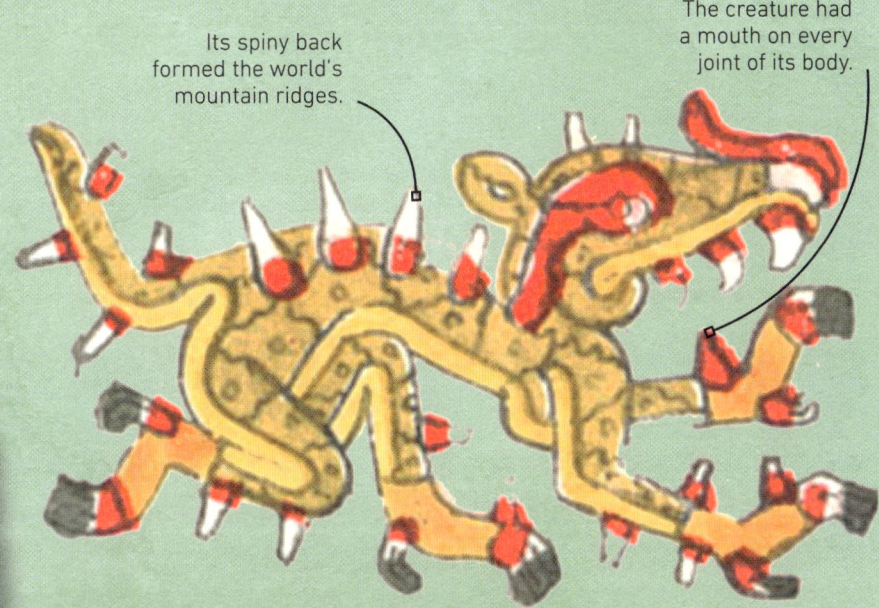

Its spiny back formed the world's mountain ridges.

The creature had a mouth on every joint of its body.

World eater
Elements of the stone depict Aztec creation myths. According to one of these, a giant crocodile called Cipactli kept destroying the worlds created by the first gods. Its face appears in the day sign for crocodile.

Moving monolith
Nearly 4 m (12 ft) across and weighing 24 tonnes, the stone was originally located in the Great Temple but has been moved many times. The Spanish buried it until, in 1790, it was found again. It is now in Mexico City's National Museum of Anthropology.

The Sun stone, displayed in a museum in 1930.

Woman thanking the divine presence in the corn she is about to cook

God in the home
People had a personal relationship with their gods. The fire in the hearth was the sacred heart of the home, represented by statues of the oldest of the fire gods, Huehueteotl.

Fire god's headdress is a brazier.

In praise of cooking
Before starting to cook, women would throw kernels of corn into the hearth to appease the ancient fire god, Huehueteotl.

Jaguar god Tepeyollotl ("Heart of the Mountains") is the protector of caves.

City protector
Every city-state had a guardian. As long as people made offerings, the deity would protect them. Huitzilopochtli, the patron god of the Aztecs (see page 33), looked after the capital, Tenochtitlan, together with his brother Tlaloc.

A god for everything

For the Aztecs, divine power was present everywhere. It manifested in the form of many different gods, but was also present in nature, including animals, the landscape, rainbows, the wind, and food. Their name for this power was *teotl*.

Headdress symbolizing the planet Venus

Evening star
Xolotl, the dark twin of the god Quetzalcoatl (see page 33), was the planet Venus as the evening star. He guarded the Sun as it went through the underworld at night.

Shape-shifting gods
Gods appeared in many guises – sometimes with human features, sometimes as animals, or a combination of both. Xolotl, a god linked to the underworld, is often depicted as a dog, but takes other forms too.

Xolotl in half-dog, half-human form

Dog-headed god
As dog, Xolotl may have brought fire and guided souls through the underworld. He was also the god of death and lightning.

Slippery skills
In one story of the creation of the Fifth Sun (see pages 34–35), Xolotl tries to escape the sacrifice of the gods by changing into a maize stalk, then a maguey plant, and finally, an axolotl.

Maize stalk   Maguey plant   Axolotl

Were-jaguars
The Aztecs believed in powerful figures called *nahualli*, who had the power to turn themselves into animals. This sculpture, created by an earlier Mesoamerican people, shows a *nahualli* transforming into a jaguar – a supernatural were-jaguar.

Beings of the dark
Nahualli were not the only supernatural beings. People believed beings called *tzitzimime* lived in the darkness. During solar eclipses, or when the world came to an end, it was thought they would swoop down from the sky to eat humans.

Necklace of human parts worn with a skirt of rattling shells

Sacred serpents

The Aztecs believed snakes were powerful creatures with links to the sky and water. The Nahuatl word for serpent – *coatl* – appears in the names of the gods Quetzalcoatl (Feathered Serpent), Mixcoatl (Cloud Serpent), and Coatlicue (She of the Serpent Skirt).

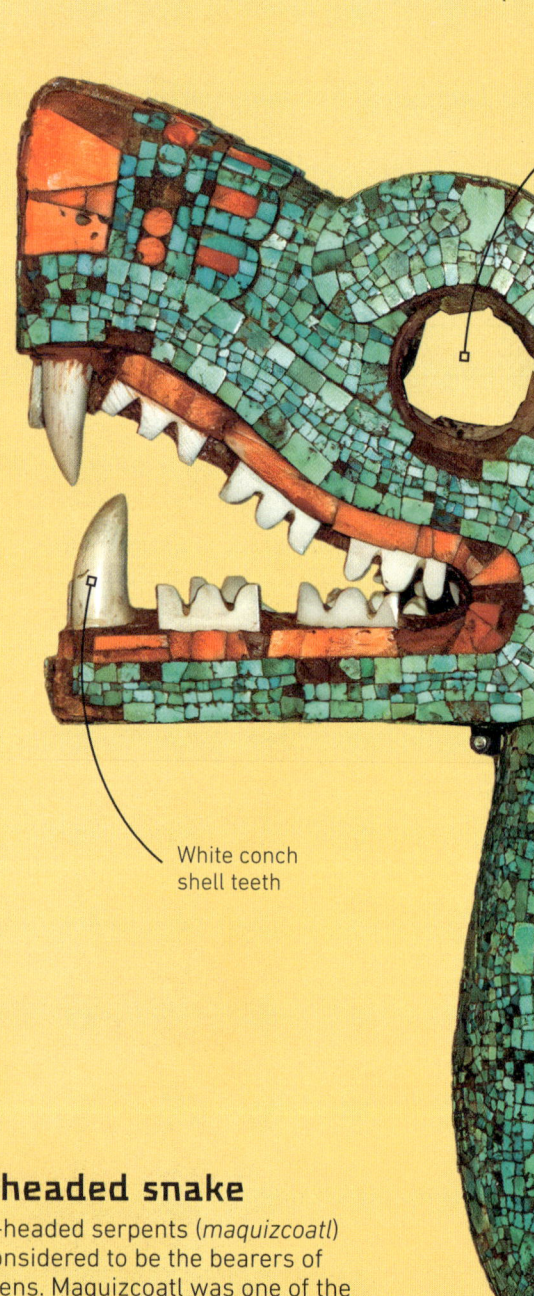

Turquoise is used to represent the serpent's scales.

Shiny stones once filled the now-empty eye sockets.

White conch shell teeth

Two-headed snake
Double-headed serpents (*maquizcoatl*) were considered to be the bearers of bad omens. Maquizcoatl was one of the names given to the supreme Aztec god Huitzilopochtli. This turquoise serpent may have been worn as a chest ornament by someone important.

Fire serpent

The *xiuhcoatl*, or fire serpent, is a powerful creature with many roles. It represents lightning, and guards the Sun on its journey. The god Huitzilopochtli wields one as a weapon, and the god of fire Xiuhtecuhtli is often shown with one, too.

The head of the serpent, with jaws open, shown in red and turquoise

Fanged carving
This stone carving shows a *xiuhcoatl* with short, clawed front feet and fearsome fangs in its mouth.

Snake companion
This symbolic illustration shows a fire serpent slithering up the back of the fire god Xiuhtecuhtli. Many gods wore the insignia of the *xiuhcoatl* on their back.

Tip of the serpent's tail

Gums, eye sockets, and snout are made from red thorny oyster shells.

Artistic interpretation of how the serpent may have been worn.

Meet the gods

Labels: Heron-feather headdress; Goggle eyes, jaguar teeth, and snake fangs; Fire serpent spear-thrower; Water-lily detail on shield; Bells around ankles

Tlaloc
Lord of Celestial Waters

- **Domains:** Rain, hail, lightning, farming
- **Superpowers:** Patron of farmers, part jaguar
- **Did you know:** Also worshipped by earlier peoples in Mesoamerica, Tlaloc is an ancient god who helped create the world. He lives on mountains, and controls how much rain falls on the land.

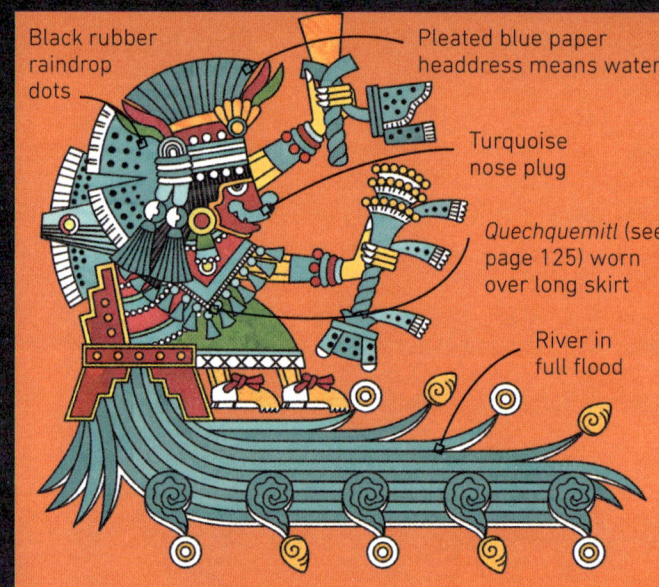

Labels: Black rubber raindrop dots; Pleated blue paper headdress means water.; Turquoise nose plug; *Quechquemitl* (see page 125) worn over long skirt; River in full flood

Chalchiuhtlicue
She of the Jade Skirt

- **Domains:** Rivers, lakes, fertility, spring
- **Superpowers:** Protector of women giving birth
- **Did you know:** A life-bringer linked to sources of fresh water needed for farming, Chalchiuhtlicue also watches over newborn babies. Many of her attributes symbolize water. She is married to Tlaloc.

Labels: Incense burner; Mask in the shape of a bird beak; Conch shell pectoral; Red and black feathered headdress; Bag full of incense

Ehecatl
God of Wind

- **Domains:** North, South, East, and West
- **Superpower:** Creating winds
- **Did you know:** Ehecatl is an aspect of Quetzalcoatl, and had an important role in the Aztec creation stories (see page 35). The conch shell on his chest symbolizes a whirlwind. Temples built for him were cone-shaped, like part of his headdress.

The Aztecs worshipped many gods. They all represented different aspects of the divine force, known as *teotl*. This gallery shows some of the best-known gods, with the attributes that define them.

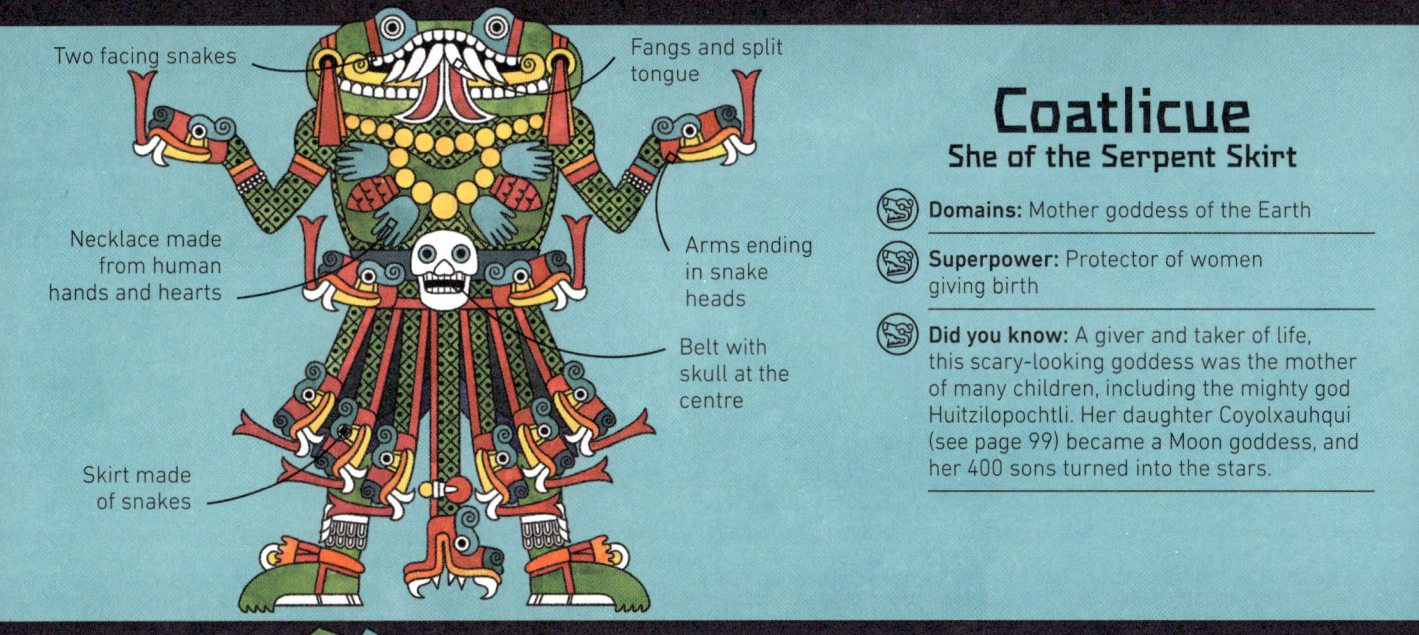

Coatlicue
She of the Serpent Skirt

- **Domains:** Mother goddess of the Earth
- **Superpower:** Protector of women giving birth
- **Did you know:** A giver and taker of life, this scary-looking goddess was the mother of many children, including the mighty god Huitzilopochtli. Her daughter Coyolxauhqui (see page 99) became a Moon goddess, and her 400 sons turned into the stars.

Two facing snakes
Fangs and split tongue
Necklace made from human hands and hearts
Arms ending in snake heads
Belt with skull at the centre
Skirt made of snakes

Mictlantecuhtli
Lord of Mictlan

- **Domains:** The underworld, the dead
- **Superpower:** Guards the souls of the dead
- **Did you know:** Mictlan, the mythical land of the dead, was full of bones. Some of these were used to create the humans who were to live in the world of the Fifth Sun, even though Mictlantecuhtli tried to stop that from happening.

Skull mask
Sacrificial knife tongue
Skeleton suit
Rosette made of pleated paper with a central cone

Mictlancihuatl
Lady of Mictlan

- **Domains:** The underworld, the dead
- **Superpower:** Swallows the stars during the day and releases them at night
- **Did you know:** She is the co-ruler of the nine regions of Mictlan. All those who did not die in battle, or by drowning, ended up in this dark realm.

She holds a knife in each hand.
Paper cone headdress matching that of her husband
Ear plug made of human bone
Necklace of human eyeballs

Meet more gods

Tlaltecuhtli
Earth Deity

- **Domains:** The Earth; all living things
- **Superpower:** Swallows the Sun at the end of each day
- **Did you know:** In one creation myth, Tlaltecuhtli becomes the first land and sky. Her curly hair turns into trees and grass. Because she represents both life and death, midwives asks for her to protect women in difficult labour.

Labels: Knife for tongue; Facing up with wide open mouth; Skulls on knees and elbows; Curly hair; Clawed feet

Xiuhtecuhtli
Fire Lord

- **Domains:** Fire, heat, volcanoes, time
- **Superpower:** Protector of Aztec rulers; rebirth of the Sun
- **Did you know:** Xiuhtecuhtli is the young fire god and one of the Lords of the Night. *Xihuitl* means both "fire" and "turquoise". He often wears a turquoise bird on his head.

Labels: Black face paint; Spear-thrower in the shape of a fire serpent

Tlazolteotl
Goddess of Filth

- **Domains:** Fertility, transformation, renewal
- **Superpower:** Restoring the balance of things
- **Did you know:** Tlazolteotl, like other Aztec goddesses, is linked to fertility and life cycles. As someone who purifies, she is celebrated at Ochpaniztli, the sweeping festival.

Labels: Spindles; Sticks to be made into brooms; Nose plug in the shape of a crescent Moon; Fine woven skirt

Some gods and goddesses are always shown with specific headdresses, objects, or symbols, while others carry different things depending on which of their roles they are personifying.

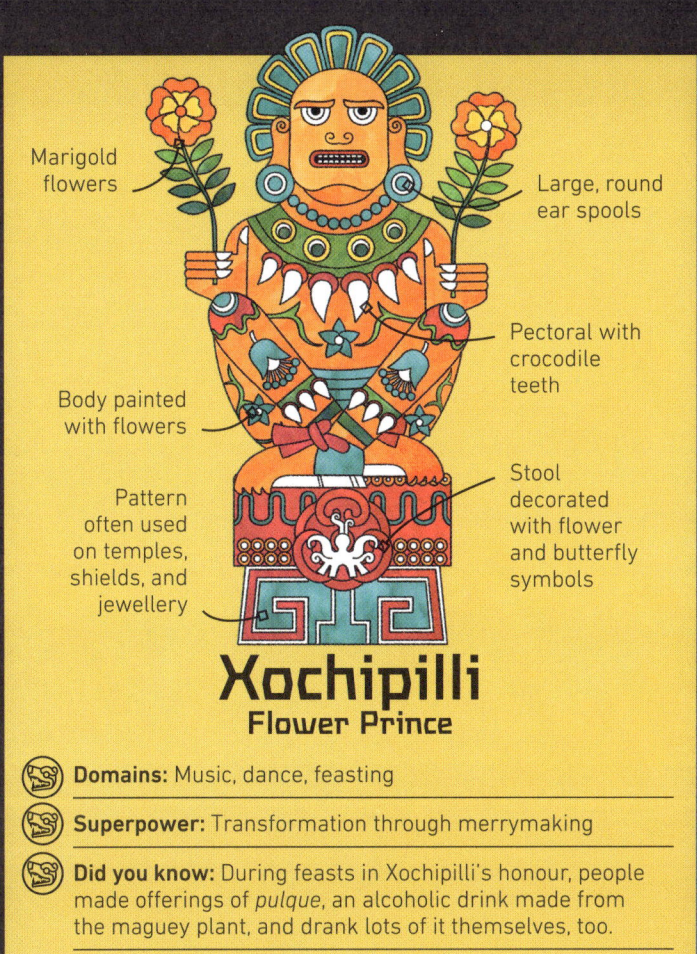

Xochipilli
Flower Prince

- **Domains:** Music, dance, feasting
- **Superpower:** Transformation through merrymaking
- **Did you know:** During feasts in Xochipilli's honour, people made offerings of *pulque*, an alcoholic drink made from the maguey plant, and drank lots of it themselves, too.

Mixcoatl
Cloud Serpent

- **Domains:** Hunting, the Milky Way and the stars
- **Superpower:** Patron of hunters; can take deer form
- **Did you know:** Mixcoatl is the father of the 400 sons of Coatlicue who turned to stars (see page 43). According to some stories, he himself was created from the Milky Way.

Yacatecuhtli
Nose Lord

- **Domains:** Trading and bartering
- **Superpower:** Protector of travelling merchants
- **Did you know:** *Yacatl* means nose, but it refers to someone who leads, or goes in front. The *pochteca*, merchants who travelled far and wide, relied on Yacatecuhtli for protection on the road.

The ritual calendar

Day signs

Every day in the 260-day ritual calendar (*tonalpohualli*) has a sign. There are 20 day signs, each associated with a deity, who gives the day its life energy (*tonalli*, see page 56). Some days were considered luckier than others.

Crocodile
Cipactli

Wind
Ehecatl

House
Calli

Lizard
Cuetzpalin

Serpent
Coatl

Death
Miquiztli

Deer
Mazatl

Rabbit
Tochtli

Water
Atl

Dog
Itzcuintli

Monkey
Ozomatli

Grass
Malinalli

Reed
Acatl

Jaguar
Ocelotl

Eagle
Cuauhtli

Vulture
Cozcacuauhtli

Movement
Olin

Flint knife
Tecpatl

Rain
Quiahuitl

Flower
Xochitl

The Aztecs measured time with two calendars: a 365-day agricultural calendar, the *xiuhpohualli* (see pages 50–51); and a 260-day ritual calendar, the *tonalpohualli*, which was used to divide time among the gods.

Counting the days

Each day in the *tonalpohualli* has a number as well as a sign. There are 20 day signs and 13 numbers, which together create 260 unique combinations, from 1 Crocodile to 13 Flower. The cog wheels show how the signs and numbers combine.

The day shown here is 1 Crocodile, which will be followed by 2 Wind, 3 House, and so on.

The numbers cycle from 1 to 13 in every *trecena*.

Thirteen days

Every 13-day period is known as a *trecena* and is named after the sign of its first day. Below is the sequence of numbers and signs in the Crocodile *trecena*.

Lucky and unlucky birthdays

The signs ruling over the day of a baby's birth were interpreted by a soothsayer and predicted the child's destiny. Babies were sometimes named after their birth day.

Two Rabbit
A person born on 2 Rabbit was likely to be a drunkard and good-for-nothing.

Nine Jaguar
A person born on 9 Jaguar was born under the sign of wild beasts, considered unlucky.

Ten Eagle
To be born on 10 Eagle, under a sign of strength and courage, was very lucky.

Fire gods

The ancient Aztec god of fire was often depicted as a toothless old man, sitting with his arms crossed over his knees. This old man god, Huehueteotl, shares attributes with the young fire lord, Xiuhtecuhtli. Many stone sculptures of the old god were buried as offerings at the Great Temple in Tenochtitlan.

The solar calendar

The veintenas

Each of the 18 *veintenas* (20-day periods) was presided over by a deity and had its own festival, celebrated with feasting, music, and dancing. The months began at the start of the farming year with Atlcahualo, meaning "the waters cease". Each *veintena* is illustrated here by the god or goddess associated with it, from a 16th-century pictorial calendar.

1. Atlcahualo
The new year began in what is our late February, calling upon the rain god, Tlaloc, for more rain.

2. Tlacaxipehualiztli
The second month was associated with the god Xipe Totec. War captives were sacrificed.

3. Tozoztontli
The month of the small vigil was dedicated to maize deities Cinteotl and Chicomecoatl (above).

Tezcatlipoca holds a flint knife.

9. Tlaxochimaco
At the offering of flowers, also known as the little feast of the dead, deities were garlanded.

10. Xocotl Huetzi
People fasted at the festival of fruit falls, also known as the great feast of the dead.

11. Ochpaniztli
This month saw rites dedicated to gods of earth and water, and the corn goddess Chicomecoatl.

12. Teotleco
Huehueteotl, the old god of fire, was celebrated at the festival for the return of the gods.

13. Tepeilhuitl
The feast of the hills in this month honoured Tlaloc and hills connected with other rain deities.

Unlucky days

At the end of the 360 days of the calendar were the five nameless days, or *nemontemi*. Here they are shown as a bald man with his tongue sticking out, wearing a flayed human skin and mask and holding an incense bag. Activity was discouraged on these days.

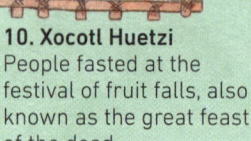

Calibrating the years

The Aztecs did not have leap years, but reset the new year to begin when the Sun rose above Mount Tepeyac, viewed from Mount Tlaloc, on 23 or 24 February. A solar observatory on the mountain (above) indicates how the sunrise was tracked.

The Aztecs also used a solar or agricultural calendar, based on the seasons, called the *xiuhpohualli*. Its 365 days were divided into eighteen 20-day *veintenas*, leaving five nameless days at the end, which were considered unlucky.

4. Huey Tozoztli
A great vigil was held to fête the maize goddess Chicomecoatl at the time of maize sowing.

5. Toxcatl
Flowers were offered to Tezcatlipoca (above) and Huitzilopochtli to ward off drought.

6. Etzalcualiztli
A festival of maize and beans honoured the abundance brought by Tlaloc, the rain god.

7. Tecuilhuitontli
In this month, the small feast of the lords, a ritual was held for saltwater goddess Huixtocihuatl.

8. Huey Tecuilhuitl
The great feast of the lords celebrated Xilonen, goddess of new maize, during the "hungry gap".

14. Quecholli
The month of precious feathers was associated with the dry season, war, and battle preparation.

15. Panquetzaliztli
This was the time to raise banners celebrating the patron god, Huitzilopochtli, and Tezcatlipoca.

16. Atemoztli
During the descent of the waters, people rejoiced at the return of the rains and fresh flowing water.

17. Tititl
This feast was dedicated to Earth mother goddess Cihuacoatl, shown here with a weaver's batten.

18. Izcalli
This festival of renewal, celebrating Xiuhtecuhtli, the young god of fire, is the last of the year.

The years

The day sign of the last day of the year gave the year its name. In practice, the year always ended on one of four signs: House, Rabbit, Reed, or Knife. These combined with the numbers 1 to 13, in 52 different combinations. This was called a bundle of years (see page 54).

The first year of the 52-year cycle is 1 House.

This is followed by 2 Rabbit.

The next year is 3 Reed.

The fourth year is 4 Knife. This will be followed by 5 House, 6 Rabbit, and so on.

Festivals

Feasts for the dead
Held in late summer, two festivals celebrated the dead. Flowers were the main feature of the first. In the second, also called "fruit falls", young men ventured up a dizzyingly tall wooden pole.

Each 20-day period (*veintena*) had its own festival, observed with feasting, music, and dance. Many were rituals to celebrate the maize cycle (see pages 116–117). Others honoured the dead, or nature.

Little Feast of the Dead
Also known as the offering of flowers, this feast involved picking flowers. Bound into garlands, they were then given to the gods. Like many festivals, the day ended with dancing.

- A priest impersonating Huitzilopochtli, the god of war
- Impersonator of skull-faced goddess Cihuacoatl, protector of women who died in childbirth
- God model surrounded by highly valued paper decorations

Great Feast of the Dead
In this festival, a pole topped by a model of a god was raised. Young men danced around it, and then tried to climb up to fetch the model.

- Youths dancing around the pole, accompanied by drums and singing
- Priest taking part in the ritual
- Strings of marigolds and wild flowers
- Musician drumming a beat

Sweeping all away

The Ochpaniztli festival, between the end of the harvest season and the start of the dry season, honoured the maize goddess. But this was also a festival of sweeping, to make temples, streets, and houses clean. Performed by goddesses, priests, and ordinary women, it was not just about hygiene, but also symbolic of fresh starts.

Broom made of straw, a symbol of the festival

Priest impersonating the maize goddess Chicomecoatl, on a temple platform

A priest dressed as one of the god Tlaloc's four helpers

Priest's headdress with goggle eyes, a symbol of Tlaloc

Tall paper house headdress decked with rosettes and streamers

Offerings of ears of maize

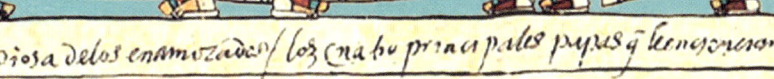

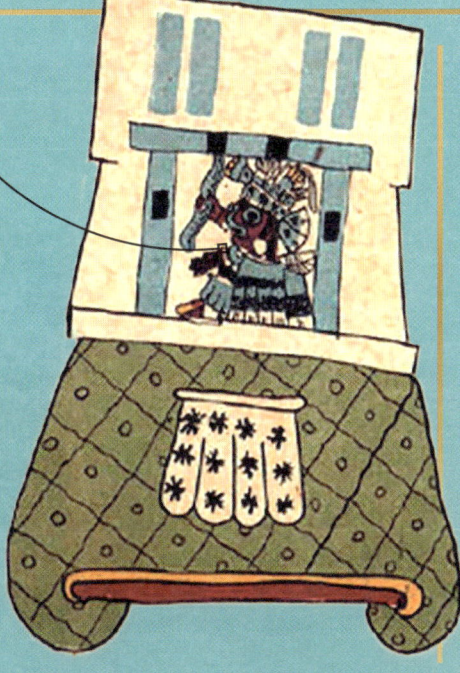

Tlaloc, the mountain-dwelling god of rain, in a hill-top temple

Mountain-top celebrations

Mountains were thought of as sacred, and home to many gods, including Tlaloc. Processions to shrines on mountains were part of several festivals, notably the festival of hills.

Paper banner painted in blue, the colour of Huitzilopochtli, raised as in battle

Winter festival

Falling near the winter solstice, the raising of banners celebrated Huitzilopochtli, in his role as a Sun god. It commemorated him leading the Aztecs to their new home. Paper banners symbolized sacrifice, bravery, and death.

New Fire ceremony

The New Fire ceremony (*xiuhmolpilli*) took place every 52 years, when the ends of the solar and ritual calendars aligned. As the Sun set, people feared the end of the world. But once they saw the blaze of sacred fire on the hilltop, signalling renewal, they knew the calendar cycle would continue.

1. Tense preparation

At dusk, people put out fires and destroy treasured possessions – nothing old can be kept. Pregnant women and children put on maguey fibre masks so they will not turn into wild animals and devour their neighbours.

Man pouring water on the family hearth

A mother-to-be puts on a protective mask. Her baby has one, too.

God figurines are thrown in the water.

Priests carry bundles of wood for the fire.

2. Priestly procession

As darkness falls, priests dressed as gods begin walking up the Hill of the Star, on the southern shores of Lake Texcoco. In complete silence, they proceed to the summit, where the ceremony takes place.

3. Lighting the fire

When the group of stars known as the Pleiades are directly above the hill, the fire must be lit. A priest uses a fire stick to create a spark in the chest of a sacrificed person. Once the kindling wood smoulders, a priest uses it to light a huge bonfire.

The flames on the temple platform can be seen by people all around the lake below.

Runner carries a blazing torch down the mountain.

Relay runner standing by to get his torch lit.

4. Light returns

Runners light bundles of sticks in the great fire, and sprint down the hill. Working in relay, they carry the flame across the land, and soon temples, palaces, and homes are lit up. The danger is over, the Sun will rise again. Everyone, dressed in new clothes, can relax, eat, and drink.

Ritual sacrifice

The Aztecs made sacrificial offerings to keep the world's energy in balance. They believed that, just as the gods gave of themselves to create the Earth, humans must give something back.

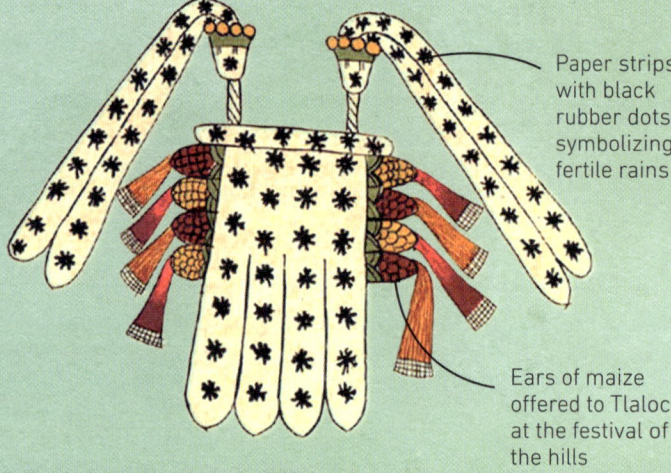

Paper strips with black rubber dots symbolizing fertile rains

Ears of maize offered to Tlaloc at the festival of the hills

Sacrificial knives
Knives for cutting through the flesh of animals and humans were called *tecpatl*. Carved from hard stone, such as obsidian or flint, they were very sharp. Many were given faces with googly eyes and toothy grins.

Making a sacrifice
Sacrifice took many forms, including giving food or flowers, burning incense, or sacrificing an animal or a human. Paper made from tree bark, a highly valued material, was used to adorn offerings.

Sun impersonator

White flint teeth fixed to an obsidian blade

Flint knife with red stripes

Blade glued into handle with sticky resin from trees and bound with plant-fibre cord

Sacred energy
A sacred energy known as *tonalli* was thought to be present in all things, circulating constantly in the world. Worshippers here offer incense, music, and their own blood to the Sun, which sends back energy in the form of light and warmth.

Bowl of fresh blood

Human heart

Statue of Mictlantecuhtli, dressed for the ceremony

Priest pouring sacrificial blood over the god statue's head

Sacrificial priest with hair worn long and matted with blood

Demanding gods

Ever since the gods sacrificed themselves to make the Sun move across the sky (see page 35), certain Aztec rituals involved human sacrifice. It took place during some festivals, and followed strict rules. This illustration shows priests bearing blood offerings to Mictlantecuhtli, the Lord of the Dead. The scale of human sacrifice was vastly exaggerated by the Spanish – possibly as fantastical travel tales or to justify their own brutal ways.

Captive dressed to personify Xipe Totec, wearing an "overall" of flayed skin

Turquoise, greenstone, and shell mosaic

Knife handle
Some ceremonial blades had handles in the shape of a deity or warrior. Carved in wood, such handles were covered in colourful mosaics.

Club lined with feathers, a symbolic, and useless, weapon

Deadly performance

One festival, Tlacaxipehualiztli (the flaying of men), was held in honour of the god Xipe Totec. In it, a prisoner of war took part in a fight with eagle and jaguar warriors. The captive was tied to a sacrificial stone and his club was lined with feathers, so the outcome was no surprise – he became an offering.

Mysterious masks

Masks were important to the Aztecs, who believed they held great power. They were worn by priests in special rituals, to "become" the god they impersonated, and were tied onto god sculptures and objects to bring them to life.

Sockets filled with sea shell and pyrite stone to resemble staring eyes

Scary skull
Made of a human skull, and with flint knives placed in the nose cavity and mouth, this mask is thought to represent Mictlantecuhtli, the god of the dead.

Flint cut into sharp edges

Knife made to look like a tongue

Ear spools made of lighter greenstone than the face

Shell carved into teeth

Treasured loot
The Aztecs appreciated masks made by peoples who lived before them in Mesoamerica. This mask – made of greenstone, which was associated with the breath of life – came from the ancient city of Teotihuacan, a place of spiritual importance. It was placed in Tenochtitlan's temple.

Bird mask
This mask has the same shape as that worn by Ehecatl, the wind god. A priest may have worn it, but it's too narrow to fit over the face so it may have been part of a feathered headdress.

A colourful mosaic of tiny mineral and shell pieces covers a wooden base.

Tezcatlipoca mask

Representing the powerful god Tezcatlipoca, this awe-inspiring mask was made from half of a human skull. Like many masks of the gods, it is largely turquoise. The Aztecs considered the stone to be divine, symbolizing life.

- Soft deerskin and plant fibres line the inside of the skull.
- Lignite, a form of coal, is used for Tezcatlipoca's black face stripes.
- Tiny turquoise tiles glued onto the skull
- Eyes made from shiny dark pyrite, encircled by conch shell
- Pieces of thorny oyster shell give the nasal cavity its red colour.
- The dead person's teeth are still attached.
- Jaw is hinged so it can open and close.
- Straps used to tie the mask onto a priest or object

Aztec society

Who's who

Aztec society worked according to a class system. Which class you were in depended mainly on who your parents were and what you did for a living, but there were some ways to gain power and status.

Class pyramid
Society could be imagined as a pyramid, with the ruler at the top, a number of wealthy and powerful nobles below, and lots of commoners at the bottom. Being a successful warrior was one way to move up the social scale.

Ruler
The ruler had ultimate responsibility for looking after his people and ensuring life continued by satisfying the gods.

Top-ranking nobles
Among the highest-ranking nobles were high priests, military leaders, and royal advisers, who had close links to the ruler.

Royal wife

Ordinary nobles
Other nobles held prestigious roles running Tenochtitlan and fighting its wars. They included constables, judges, and high-ranking warriors.

Eagle warrior · Noblewoman

Law and order
Law-breakers faced stiff punishment in courts presided over by judges and, for the most serious cases, the ruler – upholding the social hierarchy. This painting shows a man on trial for stealing jewellery.

Higher-status commoners
Merchants, skilled artisans, and warriors formed an unofficial "middle class" – they did not get noble privileges, but their work earned them special respect.

Teacher · Coppersmith · Warrior

Ordinary commoners
The vast majority of Aztecs lived simple lives, farming, hunting or gathering food, and labouring on building projects.

Male hunter · Female hunter · Porter · Farmer · Woodcutter

The ruler can be identified by his turquoise cloak and diadem.

High-ranking priests had the honour of leading ritual sacrifice ceremonies.

Canals divided Tenochtitlan's neighbourhoods.

Neighbourhood relations
Nobles had a duty of care to the commoners living in their neighbourhood, providing them with work in exchange for tribute. The city was organized into many such neighbourhoods, called *tlaxilacalli*, each with a temple and school. This 16th-century map combines Aztec and later Spanish features.

Top official | Military general | High priest

Nobleman | Constable | Governor | Noble couple

Wearing colourful, decorative clothing was one of the privileges enjoyed by nobles.

Long-distance merchant | Warrior priest | Cloth merchant | Weaver

Women who could weave intricate designs were admired for their artistry.

Wood-gatherer | Enslaved couple | Singer | Commoner women | Spinner | Boatman

Staff
Carried as a symbol of authority

Nose and lip plugs
Linked with royal power and worn by deities

Turquoise diadem
This was only worn by rulers.

Name glyph
This represents "Ilhuicamina", meaning "He Shoots Arrows at the Sky".

Ruler's cloak
Decorated with a distinctive turquoise pattern

Wearing a bright cloak with a Sun symbol, another *tlatoani* crowns Moctezuma.

Sandals
A symbol of status and nobility

Reed mat
A symbol of rulership

Royal regalia

This painting depicts the fifth Aztec ruler, Moctezuma Ilhuicamina (Moctezuma I), at his coronation. His crown and cloak – the colour of precious turquoise – as well as his jewellery and throne, signal his status as *tlatoani*.

The great speaker

Every city-state in the region had a ruler, called the *tlatoani*, meaning "one who speaks". As Tenochtitlan began to dominate, its powerful ruler earned the title *huey tlatoani* – "great speaker".

Four Rain
The era of the third Sun

One Crocodile
The coronation date (15 July)

Four Wind
The era of the second Sun

Coronation stone
When Moctezuma II became *tlatoani* in the year 11 Reed (1503 in the Western calendar), he had this stone carved to mark his coronation. It connects his reign with the five Suns (worlds) of Aztec mythology.

Four Movement
The era of the fifth Sun – the world of the Aztecs

Four Water
The era of the fourth Sun

Four Jaguar
The era of the first Sun in Aztec beliefs

Eleven Reed
The coronation year (1503)

The tlatoani speaks
Although the *tlatoani* had advisers, he had the final say on all political, military, and religious decisions. He decided when to declare war, when to make alliances, and how much tribute to demand. Here, he gathers his warriors and gives them a command.

> The good tlatoani is a protector; one who carries his subjects in his arms, who unites them, who brings them together.
>
> Florentine Codex

War array
The *tlatoani* was expected to be a brave warrior, capable of leading his troops to victory. In this illustration, a servant presents his ruler with a choice of elaborate outfits designed to intimidate the enemy.

Royal family tree

All 11 rulers were descended from the first *tlatoani*, Acamapichtli. However, the crown did not usually pass from father to son. More often it passed to a brother, uncle, or nephew.

Glyph for his name, which means "Fistful of Reeds"

Acamapichtli (r.1376–1396)

Name glyph for "Hummingbird Feather"

Huitzilihuitl (r.1397–1417)

Known in full as Moctezuma Ilhuicamina, his name glyph means "He Shoots Arrows at the Sky".

Itzcoatl (r.1427–1440)

Obsidian Serpent

Smoking Shield

Chimalpopoca (r.1418–1427)

Moctezuma I (r.1441–1469)

This curious glyph includes two parrot heads, a yellow feather, and three streams of water, meaning "Water Bird".

Tezozomoc never ruled in his own right, but fathered three rulers, one with Atotoztli and two with another wife, from Tlatelolco.

As Moctezuma I's daughter, Axayacatl's mother, and Itzcoatl's great-niece, Atotoztli was politically important, helping unite the royal family's two branches.

Atotoztli (lived c.1420–1472)

Tezozomoc (lived c.1420–1470)

Face of Water

He Who Makes Sacrifices

Axayacatl (r.1469–1481)

Tizoc (r.1481–1486)

Ahuitzotl (r.1487–1502)

Spiny Water Dog

Diadem glyph for Moctezuma Xocoyotzin, whose name means "Angry Lord the Younger"

He Descends Like an Eagle

Moctezuma II (r.1503–1520)

Cuitlahuac (r.1520)

Excrement on the Water

Cuauhtemoc (r.1521–1525)

Supreme rulers

Tenochtitlan was founded around 1325 by a leader called Tenoch. By 1376, it had become powerful enough to elect its first *tlatoani*. Between then and 1521, when the Aztec empire fell to the Spanish, the Aztecs had 11 rulers.

Some wives had higher status than others.

Hundreds of heirs
Rulers often had several wives – some noble, some not – and lots of children. At times, not everyone agreed on which son should inherit the throne. This image shows royal women in their palaces.

Choosing a new tlatoani
To become *tlatoani*, it was not enough to have royal blood. Each new ruler was selected by a group of trusted nobles, and then approved by the people. The ideal ruler had to show outstanding leadership qualities, including courage, wisdom, religious devotion, military talent, and generosity.

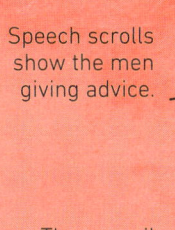

Speech scrolls show the men giving advice.

The council meets in the royal palace.

Council of Four
This illustration depicts the four noblemen entrusted with electing Moctezuma II and advising him during his reign.

Three brothers
Itzcoatl's son Tezozomoc had three sons by two different wives. All three brothers served as ruler.

Axayacatl
The youngest, Axayacatl, was chosen first. He expanded the empire north, east, and west, and crushed neighbouring Tlatelolco.

Tizoc
A weak *tlatoani*, Tizoc had this stone carved with images of his conquests – but most of these had been won by earlier rulers.

Ahuitzotl
Known for enlarging the Great Temple and increasing the empire's reach, Ahuitzotl's name glyph appears on this stone box.

Nobles and commoners

People in Aztec society belonged to one of two broad classes: the nobles (*pipiltin*) or commoners (*macehualtin*). Occasionally, a commoner could earn noble status – for example, by performing brilliantly in battle.

Well-dressed ladies
The women in this painting are preparing for a feast. As nobles, they are entitled to wear clothes with decorative designs.

Meat was eaten by nobles more often than by commoners.

Nobles
The *pipiltin* were generally noble by birth, well educated, and wealthy. They did no manual work and enjoyed many privileges, but were also expected to set a good example to the *macehualtin*.

Carrying scented flowers was a noble privilege.

Dancing lords
These noblemen wear richly coloured cloaks, knotted at the front, and precious green gems in their hair – all noble benefits.

Stone-built noble *calli* were sometimes two storeys tall.

Housing for nobles
Nobles lived in large compounds with many buildings (*calli*) of one or two rooms built around multiple courtyards.

Rules for nobles
Under Aztec law, only nobles were permitted to use fine painted pottery, drink *cacahuatl* (drinking chocolate), and wear sandals, cotton clothes, and precious gemstones. They could also receive tribute payments.

Decorated bowls were reserved for nobles.

The *cihuacoatl* is royal and wears a diadem too.

Deputy ruler
The top-ranking noble after the *tlatoani* was his deputy, the *cihuacoatl*. He ran the empire day to day, organized military operations, and served as priest in rituals honouring the Earth goddess, Cihuacoatl ("Woman Snake").

Commoners

The *macehualtin* worked the land, fished and hunted, practised a trade, or worked as entertainers. They paid tribute to the nobles, and could be required to work on public building projects.

Women were often depicted kneeling.

Female commoner

Male commoner

Rules for commoners

Commoners lived simply, going barefoot and wearing basic clothes woven from maguey fibre. They had to use plain pottery, and were not allowed to wear luxuries such as feathers.

Housing for commoners
A typical commoner compound had fewer *calli* than a noble's, built with mud-brick walls.

Commoners used undecorated bowls like this one.

A man bathes an enslaved person for ritual sacrifice.

A nobleman who governed the common folk was like their ramparts, their refuge.

Florentine Codex

Enslavement

Criminals, people who fell into debt, and some war captives could become enslaved. Most enslaved people could buy back their freedom if they paid their debt, but some were destined for ritual sacrifice.

Lords of the dance

At Tenochtitlan's royal palace, feasts were often enlivened by circular dances. At this one, noble guests, sporting fancy cloaks and feathers as displays of rank, dance around two drummers. Among them are an eagle and a jaguar warrior.

Childhood

Aztec parents were loving but strict, raising their children to be responsible, hard-working members of society. Girls and boys followed distinct paths in life.

The naming ceremony

Four days after a baby was born, a ceremony was held to name the child. It was conducted by the midwife.

A midwife holds the baby. She cuts a lock of hair from his head to be kept for when he dies.

Craft tools and a shield and four arrows symbolize a boy's future life.

Shield and arrows

Footprints show the midwife's steps around the mat as part of the ritual.

The midwife bathes the baby in a tub of water on a rush mat.

A spindle for spinning, a basket, and broom symbolize a girl's domestic future.

Becoming gendered

From birth to weaning, infants were often carried by their mothers. Babies were thought to be born without gender and became male or female through the clothes they wore and the skills they were taught.

Childhood for boys

After his birth, a boy's umbilical cord was buried, with a shield and arrows, in a place where the family had fought enemies – setting the boy up for life as a fierce warrior.

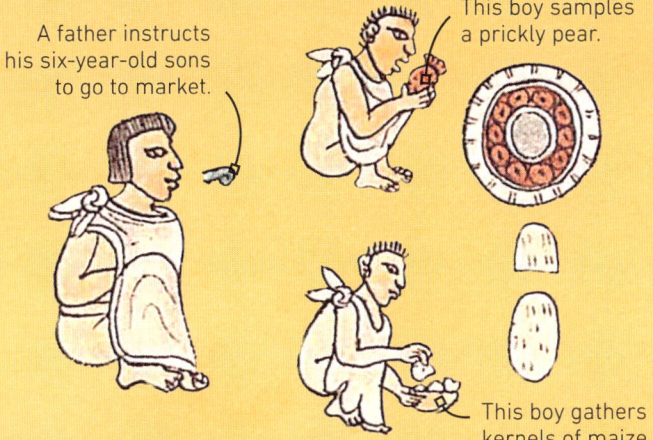

Into the world
Between the ages of four and eight, children began to dress like mini-adults and learn adult tasks. Boys were sent out into the world, wearing a cape on top and nothing underneath.

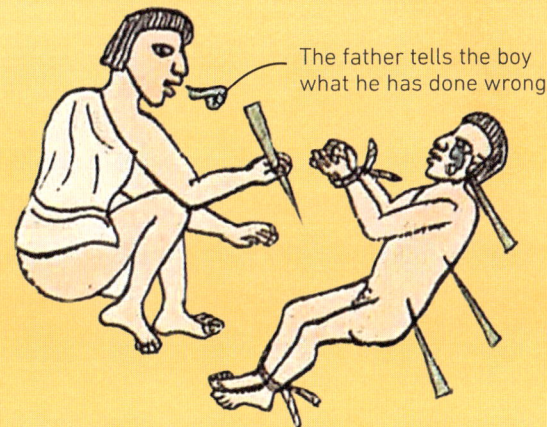

Kept in check
As children got older, from the ages of eight to 12, various punishments were used to discipline them. This boy, bound hand and foot, is being stuck with maguey thorns!

Growing responsibility
The tasks allocated to boys included going out to gather firewood and reeds. Here, a boy of around 14 brings back rushes in a flat-bottomed boat.

Childhood for girls

A girl's umbilical cord was buried under the stone used to grind grain, symbolic of a life in the home. Her childhood was devoted to learning domestic skills.

Domestic training
At the same age, girls were already being taught the essential art of spinning with a spindle. They started wearing a short tunic-like blouse, like their mother, but kept their hair short.

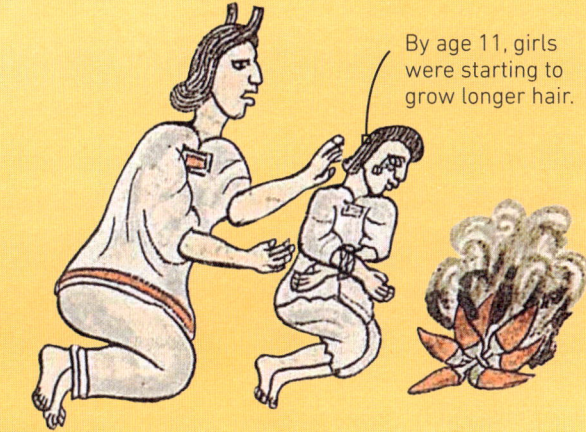

Smoked out
Girls were not exempt from punishment. This girl is being held over the smoke from a fire of chilli peppers to purge her of bad thoughts and actions.

Weaving skills
By the age of 14, when girls were on the brink of adulthood, they were skilled in the important art of weaving cloth, from cotton or maguey, to make clothes for all the family.

A boy's path

At 15, young Aztec adults were faced with different life paths, largely determined by class and gender. Boys might be sent to school, or take up an apprenticeship.

School choices

Depending on his family background, a boy might be sent to a school for nobles or a warrior school, also attended by commoners.

A father offers words of wisdom to two boys as they set off for school.

School for nobles
Noble boys were sent to the *calmecac*, a temple school run by priests. Here, a boy is received by the head priest.

The priest's long hair is tied with a white ribbon.

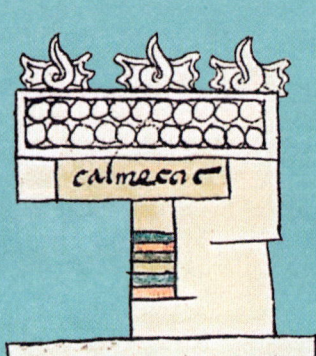

The young warrior-to-be wears a net cape.

School for commoners
Commoner boys were sent to the *telpochcalli*, or Young Men's House, to be trained in the art of war. This boy is being welcomed by the master of youths.

Boys and girls would also attend the *cuicacalli*, or House of Song, to learn ritual singing and dancing.

Apprenticeships

Not all boys were sent to school. Some of them learned a skilled trade instead. In these scenes, boys are apprenticed to various artisans. Skills were often passed from father to son.

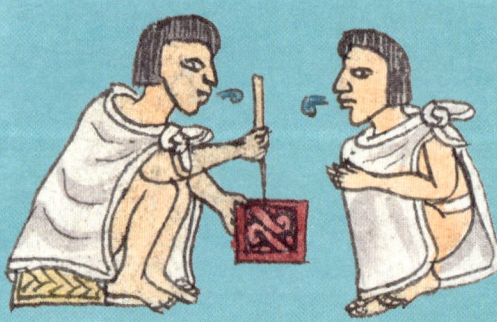

Scribe
A scribe instructs his son in the use of a painting tool. He teaches him how to mix ink and charcoal to draw people and flowers.

Featherworker
A son helps his father prepare colourful feathers for a headdress, using a needle threaded with maguey fibre.

The commoner path

Boys at the *telpochcalli* had to learn self-discipline and help with temple rituals. The boys also did manual labour, such as digging canals and making mud bricks.

The noble path

For boys at the *calmecac*, life was austere. The boys stayed awake at night for rituals and frequently fasted. But they also learned arts such as astronomy.

Temple duties
Boys carry wood from the forests to keep the fires burning in the temple, and fresh green boughs to decorate it.

Ritual sweeping
Boys perform ritual sweeping and gather bundles of reeds for ceremonial rites in the temple.

Faces are painted black with soot.

Setting off for war
A *telpochcalli* boy is sent off to war, loaded with provisions and arms. He carries a shield, arrows, and provisions, lashed to a carrying frame, and holds an obsidian-studded spear as a staff.

Star symbol represents what the priest sees.

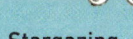

Starry sky

Stargazing
The boys learned from the head priest, who is seen here observing the stars in the night sky.

Community service
As part of his duties, a boy in a canoe brings sods of earth to the temple for its repair.

A smear of red on his cheek identifies this boy as a novice priest.

Stones to the temple
Like the commoner boy, a young noble transports stones in a canoe for temple repairs.

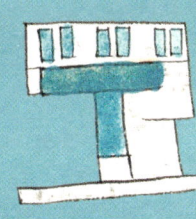

Goldsmith
A skilled goldsmith blows into a brazier with a pipe to raise the heat of the charcoal and melt gold for casting, watched by his son.

Stonecutter
A lapidary instructs his son in the art of cutting and polishing gemstones, using a cane tool to polish greenstone beads.

Swing time
Despite strict moral codes, this sculpture of two girls on a swing suggests that life was not all hard work in Mesoamerica. The figures are from the Totonac culture on the Gulf Coast, which was dominated by and paid tribute to the Aztecs from the late 1400s.

Festival of growth
Children were encouraged to grow up fast. At the annual Izcalli festival of growth, they were physically stretched by the neck, had their ears pierced, and were offered their first taste of *pulque* (an alcoholic drink made from maguey sap).

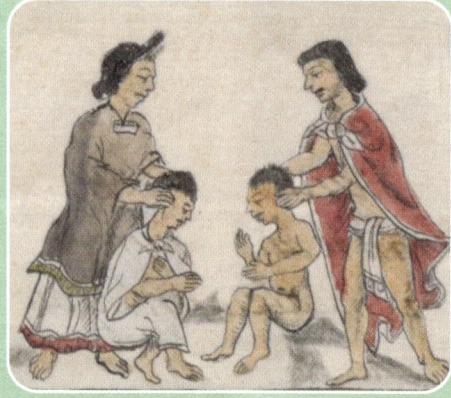

Neck stretching
A girl and a boy have their necks stretched by their parents to help them grow up, so they can assist with adult work.

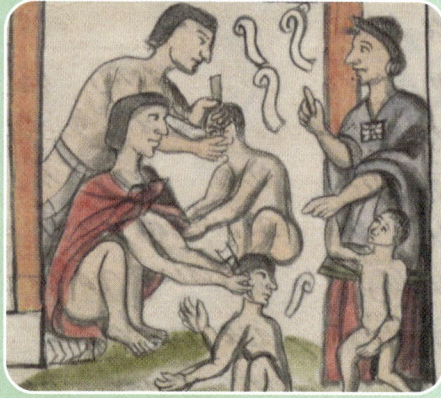

Ear piercing
A mother accompanies her children as they have their ears pierced with maguey thorns.

Tasting pulque
Children are offered a cup of *pulque*, an alcoholic drink made from the maguey plant, under strict adult supervision.

3. Tying the knot
The couple, seated on a rush mat, seal the marriage by tying the knot. The matchmaker performs the ritual.

Copal is burned as incense to honour the fire god Xiuhtecuhtli.

The man reminds the couple of their duty to bear strong children.

The bride's *huipilli* is tied in a knot with the groom's cape.

2. Elders' advice
An older couple offer advice on married life, while enjoying the wedding feast.

A bowl of turkey legs and a basket of tamales is served to guests.

Pulque, served in a distinctive jar, loosens the guests' tongues.

The bride's red face paint may be a tribute to the fertility goddess Tlazolteotl.

Torch-bearers carry blazing pine torches to illuminate the bridal procession.

1. Bridal procession
The bride-to-be is carried to the ceremony by a matchmaker, in a torchlit procession.

A girl's life
Having learned domestic skills – how to spin, weave, and make tortillas – from early childhood, girls were married young. Starting at the bottom, this image depicts the stages of a wedding ceremony.

Growing pains

Children and young people were expected to be productive members of society. Girls embarked on adult life from their late teens, getting married and taking on domestic duties.

Spinners and weavers

As expert spinners and weavers, women clothed their families as well as contributing to the wealth of their own household and the Aztec empire. They produced valuable textiles for tribute, trade, and diplomatic gift-giving.

Natural materials

Plants, feathers, and animal skins and fur were all used to make cloth, though some materials were reserved for nobles. Textiles spun from maguey or cotton were woven with feather down and rabbit fur for softness, warmth, and colour.

Maguey plant

Animal skins
While commoner warriors wore real animal skins, nobles wore "jaguar pelts" made of feathers.

Maguey
Cloth woven from maguey fibres was worn by commoners.

Feathers
Signifying high status, feathers added colour and shine to elite warrior costumes.

Cotton
Raw cotton, sent in bales as tribute, was transformed into fine cloth worn by nobles.

Quilt protection

Combining raw and woven cotton, women produced quilted armour for warriors. The padding was light and comfortable, but thick enough to deflect arrows.

Quilted tunic worn by a warrior

Red leather trim

Puffy raw cotton was sandwiched between layers of woven cotton cloth.

Weaving wealth

Noblemen could have many wives. The textiles these women wove could be exchanged for other valuables or given as ceremonial gifts, bringing the family wealth and respect. The more wives, the wealthier the household.

This woman's tunic-like blouse (*huipilli*), decorative skirt, and sandals indicate her wealth and high status.

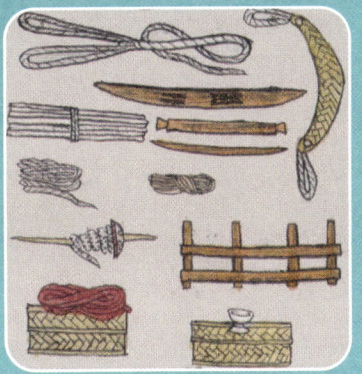

Spinners from birth
Every baby girl received a set of spinning and weaving tools at birth, representing her domestic future.

A good woman

For the Aztecs, a perfect woman had to be able to spin and weave beautifully to bring honour to herself and her family, and fulfil her role in the home. Her training began the day she was born.

The spindle tip rests in a small bowl, giving the spinner more control.

Spinning
Girls learned to spin early, developing the skills to spin cotton, feathers, and animal hair into thread with a spindle.

The weaver pushes thread into place with a batten.

Weaving
Women wove thread into cloth on a backstrap loom, with one end tied around the waist and the other tied to a pole.

Well-dressed noblewomen carrying textiles they have woven

Warriors

Waging war was central to the Aztec way of life, and warriors – both nobles and commoners – held a special place in society. Every boy dreamed of becoming a hero on the battlefield.

Captives not casualties
In Aztec warfare, the main aim was not to kill the enemy, but to take captives and force the other side into submission.

- An Aztec warrior takes an enemy captive.
- The dominant warrior appears larger than the captive.

Rich rewards
The ruler rewarded successful warriors with fine clothing, jewellery, titles, and even farmland with people to tend it.

- Fancy cloaks displayed rank and status.

- High-ranking warriors carried fine feather shields.
- Both warriors carry the *macuahuitl*, a club with sharp obsidian blades.

Climbing the ranks
Success in battle was a way of climbing the social ladder. Commoners admitted to the Order of Eagles and Jaguars achieved noble status.

- Jaguar and eagle warriors dressed as those animals.

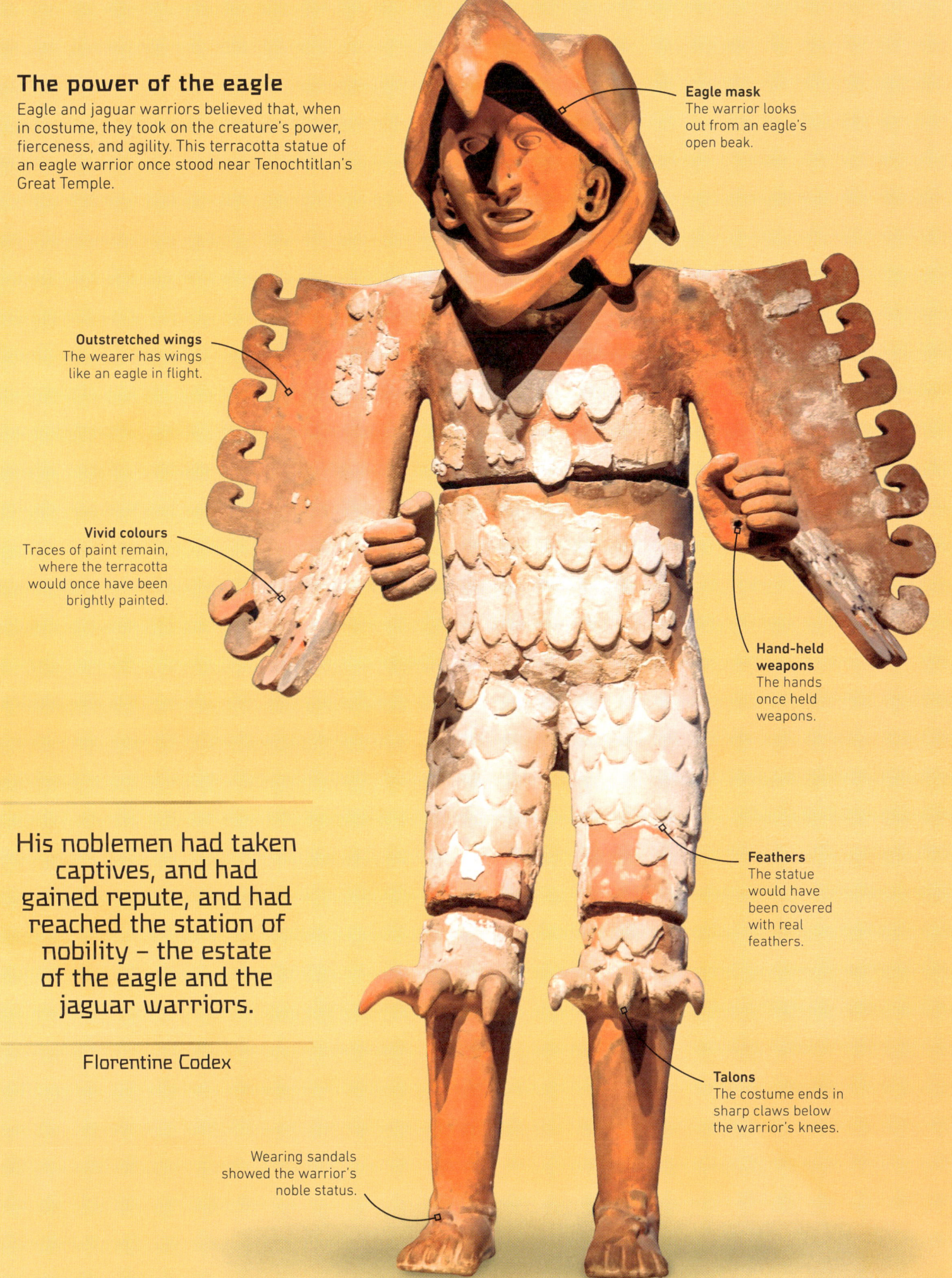

The power of the eagle
Eagle and jaguar warriors believed that, when in costume, they took on the creature's power, fierceness, and agility. This terracotta statue of an eagle warrior once stood near Tenochtitlan's Great Temple.

Eagle mask
The warrior looks out from an eagle's open beak.

Outstretched wings
The wearer has wings like an eagle in flight.

Vivid colours
Traces of paint remain, where the terracotta would once have been brightly painted.

Hand-held weapons
The hands once held weapons.

Feathers
The statue would have been covered with real feathers.

Talons
The costume ends in sharp claws below the warrior's knees.

Wearing sandals showed the warrior's noble status.

> His noblemen had taken captives, and had gained repute, and had reached the station of nobility – the estate of the eagle and the jaguar warriors.
>
> Florentine Codex

Warrior ranks

Aztec warriors won promotion by capturing enemy prisoners. Each additional captive earned them greater renown, rewards, and privileges, including the right to wear increasingly elaborate battle dress.

Career path of a successful warrior

Warriors were ranked by the number of captives they had taken, allowing commoners to climb the ranks. However, the very highest ranks (five captives or more) were only open to noble-born warriors.

Tlamani
By taking one captive, a warrior achieved the rank of *tlamani*, entitling him to a patterned cloak.

- A flowered cloak was worn in public as a badge of honour.
- A one-captive warrior was awarded a club-like weapon and a plain shield.

Cuextecatl
With two captives, a warrior could wear a striped body suit, conical hat, and sandals.

- A two-captive warrior's cloak is plain orange with a red border.
- The shield, striped to match the suit, has feather tassels.
- Sandals were worn from this rank up.

Papalotl
A three-captive warrior wore quilted cotton armour and a *papalotl* (butterfly) ornament on his back.

- This cloak has symbols of Ehecatl, god of wind.
- Feather ornament in the shape of a butterfly

Early training
After learning how to fight and use weapons at warrior school, novice warriors gained real-world experience by accompanying seasoned warriors to the battlefield. There they learned how to work together to capture a prisoner.

Field experience
Novices' first taste of war was as porters. They carried equipment and learned by observing more experienced warriors.

The first captive
The moment a youth took his first captive, he officially joined the military ranks and was allowed a warrior's hairstyle (see pages 128–129).

Cloak with diagonal design worn by four-captive warrior

Jaguar pelt design made with feathers

Cuauhocelotl
The first noble rank, eagle or jaguar warriors wore magnificent animal costumes and feather headdresses.

Quetzal feathers were a mark of high status.

Hairdo bound in a tassel

Otontin
Five-captive warriors wore a green body suit, showy jewellery, and an impressive feather back ornament.

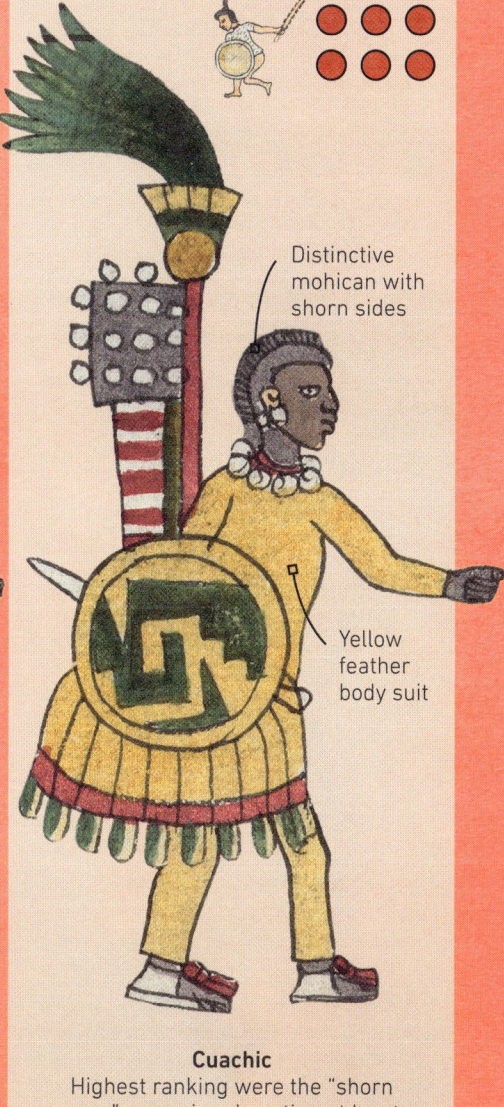

Distinctive mohican with shorn sides

Yellow feather body suit

Cuachic
Highest ranking were the "shorn ones" – warriors boasting at least six captives and 20 brave deeds.

Warrior leaders

Tlacateccatl

The *tlacateccatl* ("cutter of men") was the commanding general. He was in charge of the *tlacatecco*, a military district of Tenochtitlan. He was also one of four top-ranking noblemen who advised the ruler.

Tlacochcalcatl

The *tlacochcalcatl* ("keeper of the house of darts") was a general. He had important legal and administrative duties and was also one of the council of four. His tasselled feather headdress signified nobility.

These four mighty warriors were all Aztec generals. Off the battlefield, they served as trusted officials. Leading their men into the fray, their magnificent outfits were guaranteed to intimidate the enemy.

Huitznahuatl

The *huitznahuatl* ("thorn speech") wore a feathered back ornament used – like all such banners – for signalling to troops. He also served as a constable who helped the ruler decide on difficult legal cases.

Ticocyahuacatl

The *ticocyahuacatl* ("keeper of the bowl of fatigue") wore a costume and banner similar to that of a *cuachic* warrior, but had a different hairstyle. The design on his banner resembled a starry sky.

Battle plans
When preparing for war, the ruler first sent spies to explore the enemy territory and draw a map showing the safest routes of attack. He and his generals used this to plan their campaign.

Weapons and armour
At long range, warriors fought with arrows, slingshots, and spears. In close combat, they wielded clubs and axes. For protection, they relied on light, padded cotton armour and circular wooden shields, often adorned with feathers.

Field tactics
Going into battle, the most fearsome warriors led the charge, followed by experienced fighters, then novices. Generals directed their men by waving their feather banners, blowing whistles, and beating drums.

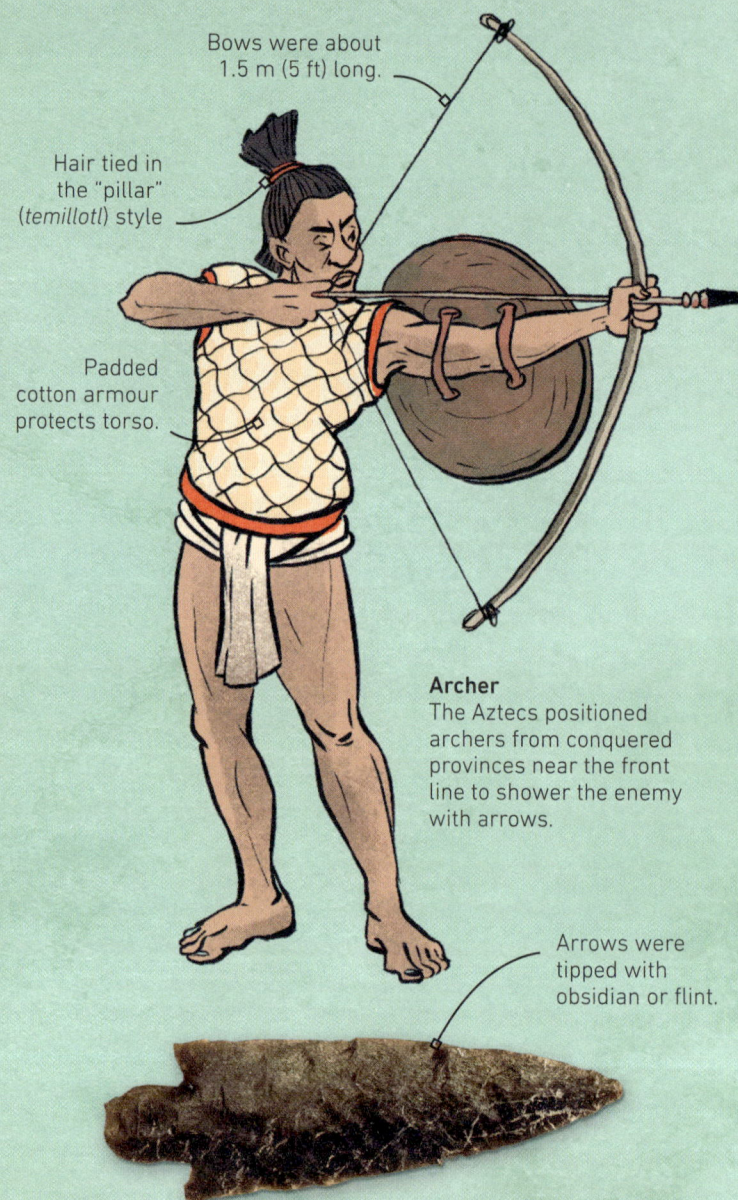

Bows were about 1.5 m (5 ft) long.

Hair tied in the "pillar" (*temillotl*) style

Padded cotton armour protects torso.

Archer
The Aztecs positioned archers from conquered provinces near the front line to shower the enemy with arrows.

Arrows were tipped with obsidian or flint.

Setting fire to the enemy's temple

Fiery conquest
Warriors attacking a city-state tried to reach and burn its main temple, a sign of victory.

Conch shell trumpet
A blast on a conch shell trumpet, at dawn, signalled the start of the fighting.

Flowery wars
Not all wars were fought to conquer. In "flowery wars", the Aztecs fought another city-state at a pre-arranged time and place to collect captives they could bring home for ritual sacrifice.

One of four surviving Aztec featherwork shields, with a typical "stepped fret" design

Club-like weapon studded with obsidian blades

Spears were wooden with obsidian tips.

Spear-thrower helps spear travel further

Eagle warrior
Skilled, high-ranking warriors fought hand-to-hand, wielding a lethal, club-like weapon called a *macuahuitl*.

Shield used to barge or block opponents

Eagle suit made of cotton and feathers shows high status of wearer.

Colourful feather body suit

Cuachic warrior
Top-ranking "shorn" warriors, famed for their bravery, hurled spears at the oncoming enemy.

Ceremonial spear-thrower (*atlatl*) of wood, shell, and hammered gold

Warfare and weapons

Aztec warfare was a combination of careful planning, showmanship, and courageous combat. All warriors fought on foot, relying on good coordination to outwit the enemy and break through their ranks.

Priests

Aztec priests communicated between the people and the gods and goddesses. They had a duty to perform rituals at the right time according to the ritual calendar (see pages 46–47), to satisfy the deities and ensure that Aztec life continued to flourish.

Very Important Priests
Priests' special relationship with the gods gave them power and prestige. Many served as teachers, and the most important as royal advisers.

Students learning from a priest

Looking priestly
Spotting a priest was easy: they painted their skin black with soot, smeared red blood on their temples, and never washed or cut their hair. This look symbolized their close connection with the gods.

Gifts of blood for the gods

Priests' hair became long and matted.

An incense burner shaped like the goddess Xilonen, used for copal.

Priestly life
A priest's life was tough. Priests had to work long hours, wake often at night for temple rituals, and pierce their own ears and tongues to offer blood to the gods.

Scented smoke wafts up to the gods.

Essential incense
Every Aztec ritual involved burning copal, a sticky tree resin. Its sweet, smoky scent was believed to nourish the gods.

A priest holding a censer ladles burning incense into a brazier.

Typical activities
To keep the gods happy, priests made daily offerings of incense and blood, as well as organizing regular public festivals.

Divine women

Priests in Aztec society were men. However, women who worked as midwives and healers in the community also had powerful roles communicating with deities.

— A female healer chanting to the gods

— The priest wears a mask.

Priestly roles

Temple priests developed special areas of knowledge and activity, such as reading the stars and planets, interpreting calendars, going to war, or performing in public ceremonies.

Deity impersonator
Impersonators acted as gods during rituals. This statue shows a priest assuming the identity of Xipe Totec, dressed in a human skin symbolizing sacrifice and new life.

Elaborate feathers signal priest's high rank.

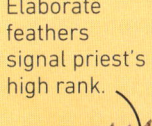

Head priest
The head priest oversaw the running of the temple, and had the honour of performing ritual sacrifices.

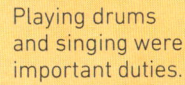

— Playing drums and singing were important duties.

Warrior priest
Some priests trained to fight. Warrior priests had their own ranking system based on the number of captives they took.

This priest has taken five captives.

— A soothsayer tells a mother her baby's destiny.

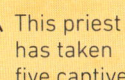

Soothsayer
Soothsayers read the stars and interpreted ritual calendars. They advised which days were lucky or unlucky.

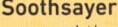

Merchants and artisans

Two groups, merchants and artisans, had a higher status than other commoners. Merchants became wealthy by trading luxury goods, while artisans earned respect for their specialist skills.

Artisans
Aztec artisans created fine temples and sculptures, produced luxury items for trade, and made the elaborate adornments and ceremonial objects required for sacred rituals, warfare, and noble living.

Stonecutter
A stonecutter's work involved quarrying, cutting stone to size, building noble houses, and carving sculptures.

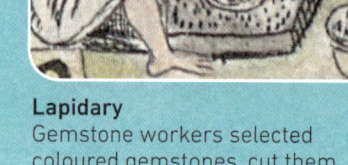

Sand is used to smooth the stone's surface.

A string of polished beads

Lapidary
Gemstone workers selected coloured gemstones, cut them to size, then polished them to a shine to make jewellery.

Merchants
Merchants had an important role in expanding the Aztec empire and bringing wealth to Tenochtitlan. They gathered information about other city-states, made trading contacts, and collected tribute for the empire.

Merchants travelled by foot, carrying goods on their backs.

A decorated staff honouring Yacatecuhtli, the protector god

A hard life
Merchants spent months on the road, far from home, and could be attacked for their precious cargo.

Straps around the head helped to support heavy loads.

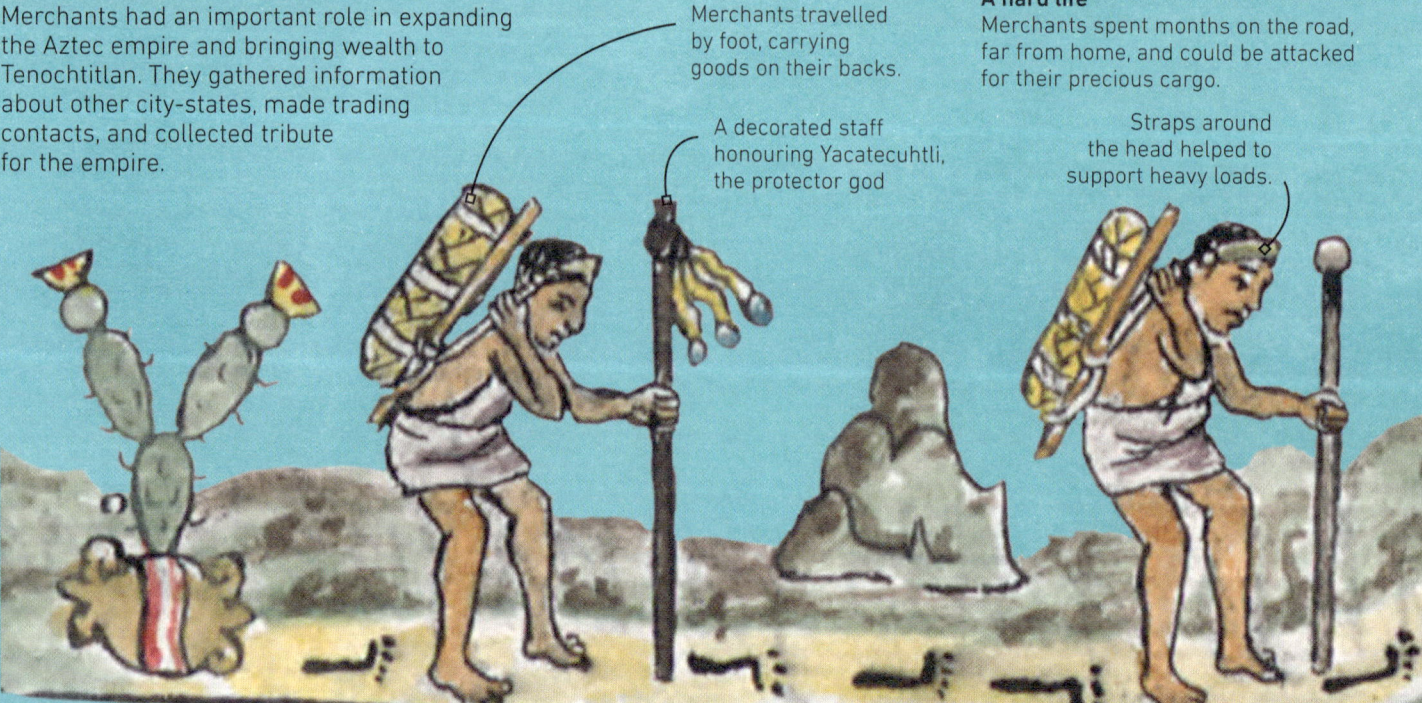

This man uses a blowpipe to fan the fire.

Goldsmith
Skilled goldsmiths melted the metal over hot coals, then poured it into a mould to cool and harden into ornaments.

The design is painted onto the hardened cloth.

Featherworker
Fine featherworkers painted designs before glueing or tying exotic feathers – sometimes dyed – into place to make adornments.

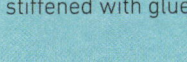

Cotton is laid on a maguey leaf and stiffened with glue.

Carpenter
A good carpenter knew how to cut and join pieces of wood so they fitted together perfectly, to build simple wooden houses.

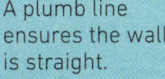

A plumb line ensures the wall is straight.

Mason
Skilful masons were experts at joining mud bricks together with mortar to make perfectly smooth adobe walls.

Aztec merchants travelling in disguise have copied the local hairstyle.

This person's hairstyle and colourful cape are distinctive to their region.

Merchants were nicknamed "mice" because of their reputation for being sneaky spies.

Merchant spies
Long-distance merchants acted as spies for the empire, secretly listening for information to help the Aztec ruler plan conquests.

The city on the lake

Tenochtitlan

When the Aztecs founded their city in 1325, they began building on a small island off the marshy lake shore. Soon, the city expanded by merging with nearby Tlatelolco island. By 1519, Tenochtitlan was a large and well-organized city of around 50,000 people, with more visiting every day.

Surrounded by water

With water all around it, Tenochtitlan was criss-crossed by canals and linked to other cities on the shore by causeways. Canoes were the main means to transport goods.

Dyke, known as the serpent wall (*coatepantli*), built to protect the city from flooding and keep the saltier water of the main lake out

The busiest of the city's markets is at Tlatelolco (see pages 106–107).

Causeway leading to Tepeyacac, a mountain settlement on the lake shore

Tlatelolco has its own sacred area with many temples.

The main causeway leading to Tlacopan, an allied city-state, also carries freshwater from the mainland through an aqueduct.

Housing

Outside the sacred centre, families lived in small houses in one of the city's four main districts. Noble houses were built of stone, commoner houses of mud brick or wattle and daub.

Clean streets

Sweeping dirt away from streets, squares, and houses was a public duty, carried out by a thousand cleaners. It kept the city neat and tidy, staved off disease, and had a religious meaning of renewal too.

Iztaccihuatl ("white lady"), according to legend a princess turned into a sleeping volcano

Popocatepetl ("smoking mountain"), an active volcano

Tenochtitlan's sacred and ceremonial centre (see pages 96–99)

Artificial islands known as *chinampas* created for farming (see pages 112–113)

Causeway leading to Iztapalapa and the Hill of the Star, where the New Fire ceremony (see pages 54–55) was held.

Ordinary people live in outer neighbourhoods, in houses along canals.

Walled precinct

The sacred area is shown as it was at Moctezuma II's time. Each temple was thought of as home of the god worshipped there. Just outside the walls, the rulers built their palaces.

❶ Temple of Tezcatlipoca
Priests working here often cover their bodies in black soot and hold obsidian mirrors during rituals.

❷ Local marketplace
Tenochtitlan has its own market, but it is much smaller than the market at Tlatelolco (see pages 106–107).

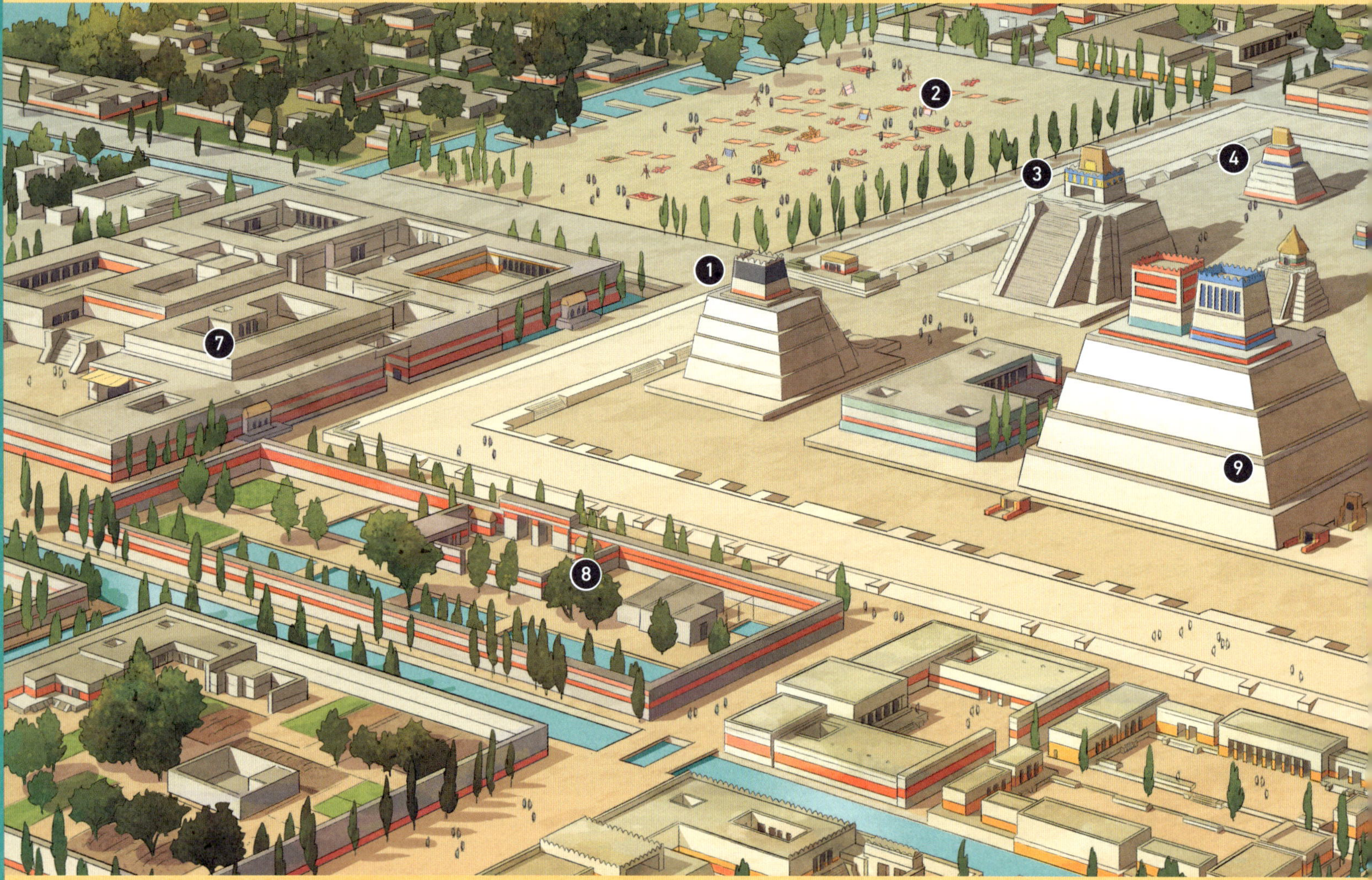

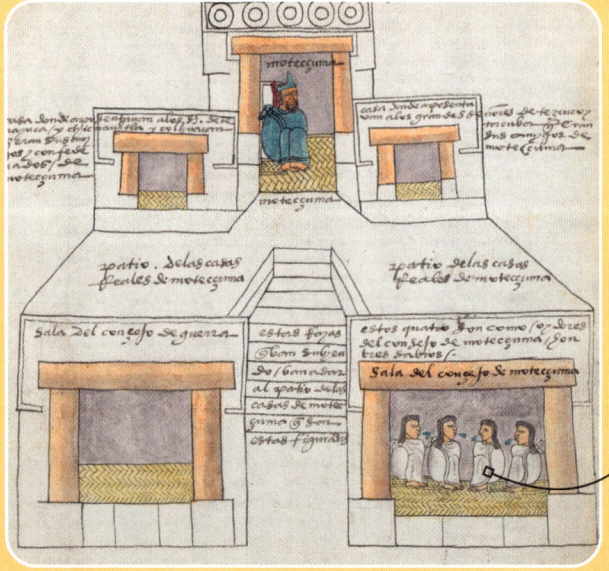

❼ Palace of Moctezuma II
Built in 1502, this vast palace is where Moctezuma II lives (in the room at the top) and receives advisers, priests, and dignitaries. It is a maze of halls, corridors, gardens, and a hundred baths, all looked after by hundreds of servants.

Nobles gathering for a council in a palace hall

❽ Moctezuma's zoo
To impress and entertain, Moctezuma II keeps exotic birds and animals in lush gardens, with aviaries and fish pools.

③ Temple of Tonatiuh
This is the temple of the Fifth Sun. Between it and the Temple of Tezcatlipoca lie disc-shaped Sun stones.

④ Temple of Xipe Totec
Flayed skins worn in rituals by impersonators of this god are stored in stone boxes held in the temple.

⑤ Ball court
Ceremonial ballgames are played here. In front of the court stands a large rack of sacrificial victims' skulls.

⑥ Temple of Quetzalcoatl
In his form as wind god, Ehecatl–Quetzacoatl dwells and is worshipped in a round temple where winds can swirl.

⑨ Great Temple
The main temple is a twin temple dedicated to city patron Huitzilopochtli and rain god Tlaloc (see pages 98–101).

⑩ Eagle warriors' house
Statues of warriors and Mictlantecuhtli, the god of death, guard the house where elite eagle warriors meet.

⑪ Merchants' complex
Wealthy merchants (*pochteca*) have their own space. It includes a shrine to their god, Yacatecuhtli.

⑫ Guarded gates
The walled precinct has four entrances, one for each cardinal direction. This is the North gate.

Sacred centre

In the middle of Tenochtitlan was a walled area, full of large temples and grand open spaces. This was the city's ceremonial heart and, except for special events, only rulers, nobles, priests, and elite warriors had access.

Twin temples 1
The two main protector gods of Tenochtitlan had one temple each, shown in this codex illustration (see page 152). Only priests could enter the indoor spaces, where images of the gods were kept.

Sacred guardians 3
Large serpent heads at the bottom of each set of stairs keep watch over the temple.

Temple of Tlaloc
Temple of Huitzilopochtli

The platform in front of the twin temples was used for rituals and ceremonies.

Stairs lead up to the platform.

Revealing excavations 2
Long hidden beneath modern Mexico City, the layers of temple steps only came to light in 1978. The illustration is cut away to reveal the layers. During excavations, thousands of offerings were found inside.

First temple
The original temple was built by Acamapichtli.

Layered pyramid
The first temple was built soon after the founding of the city in 1325. After that, the next rulers built new structures on top of the existing one, so the temple grew taller and taller. In the end, there were seven layers. The last one was built by Moctezuma II. Today, only parts remain.

The Great Temple

In the centre of Tenochtitlan stood an enormous step pyramid. At the top of the tall stairs was a platform with two temples – one dedicated to Tlaloc, god of rain, and one to the city's patron, Huitzilopochtli, god of war and the Sun.

Temple decorations

Looming over the square below, the temple appeared stern and imposing. But it had colourful statues and carvings, all with deep religious meaning.

4 Offer holder
This statue sat on the platform of the first temple. It is believed that his bowl was used to receive offerings. This type of statue also appears in temples of cultures older than the Aztecs, such as the Maya.

Traces of red pigment show the sculpture was painted.

Wall of skulls

Skull racks (*tzompantli*) stood near the temple to display the heads of sacrificial victims. This one displays carved stone skulls. Others held real skulls of sacrificed people. Strung between wooden poles in great numbers, they made a clattering noise in the wind.

Gold bells and feathers adorn her face.

Fighting siblings 5
Coyolxauhqui was Huitzilopochtli's sister. When she heard that her mother, Coatlicue, was pregnant, she tried to kill her. But then Huitzilopochtli was born, armed to the teeth, and killed his sister. This stone, depicting the dead Coyolxauhqui, was placed at the temple's base.

Coyolxauhqui's legs and arms broke off when her body was thrown off a mountain.

Belt with a skull attached to it.

Coronation ceremony

In 1503, Tenochtitlan's Great Temple was the setting for the coronation of Moctezuma II, the last great Aztec ruler. Priests, officials, nobles, warriors, and ordinary people gathered to watch.

Coronation of Moctezuma II
Becoming the new ruler was a long process. After spending several days alone to prepare for his new role, Moctezuma heard speeches from elders, intended to guide his actions. Then came the time to climb the pyramid of the Great Temple for the ritual coronation.

Moctezuma dressed in a luxurious cape and a feathered arm decoration

Priest walking up towards the temple of Tlaloc. Commoners were not allowed up here.

A priest and ruler handing the ruler's diadem to Moctezuma

1. Royal outfit
Just before the coronation ceremony, Moctezuma changed from the simple clothes he had worn while fasting alone. Dressed in an exquisite turquoise cape, and with feathers symbolizing his link to the god Huitzilopochtli, he received the turquoise diadem, marking his role as ruler.

2. Sacrifice to the Sun god
As new ruler, Moctezuma made a sacrifice of a quail to Huitzilopochtli, on the platform outside the god's temple.

Feather headdress linking Moctezuma to the divine power of Huitzilopochtli

Large turquoise gemstone

3. Warrior king
After the coronation ceremony at the temple, Moctezuma had to show himself a worthy ruler by going off to war and returning with captives. He came back, successful, dressed as the warrior god, Huitzilopochtli.

Exquisitely woven and bejewelled loincloth

Priests assisting at the ceremony, burning incense

Standard-bearers stand in position along the sides.

4. Afterparty
The coronation events ended with Moctezuma giving a grand feast in his palace. Nobles and eagle and jaguar warriors were given gifts, and danced to the drumbeat played by musicians.

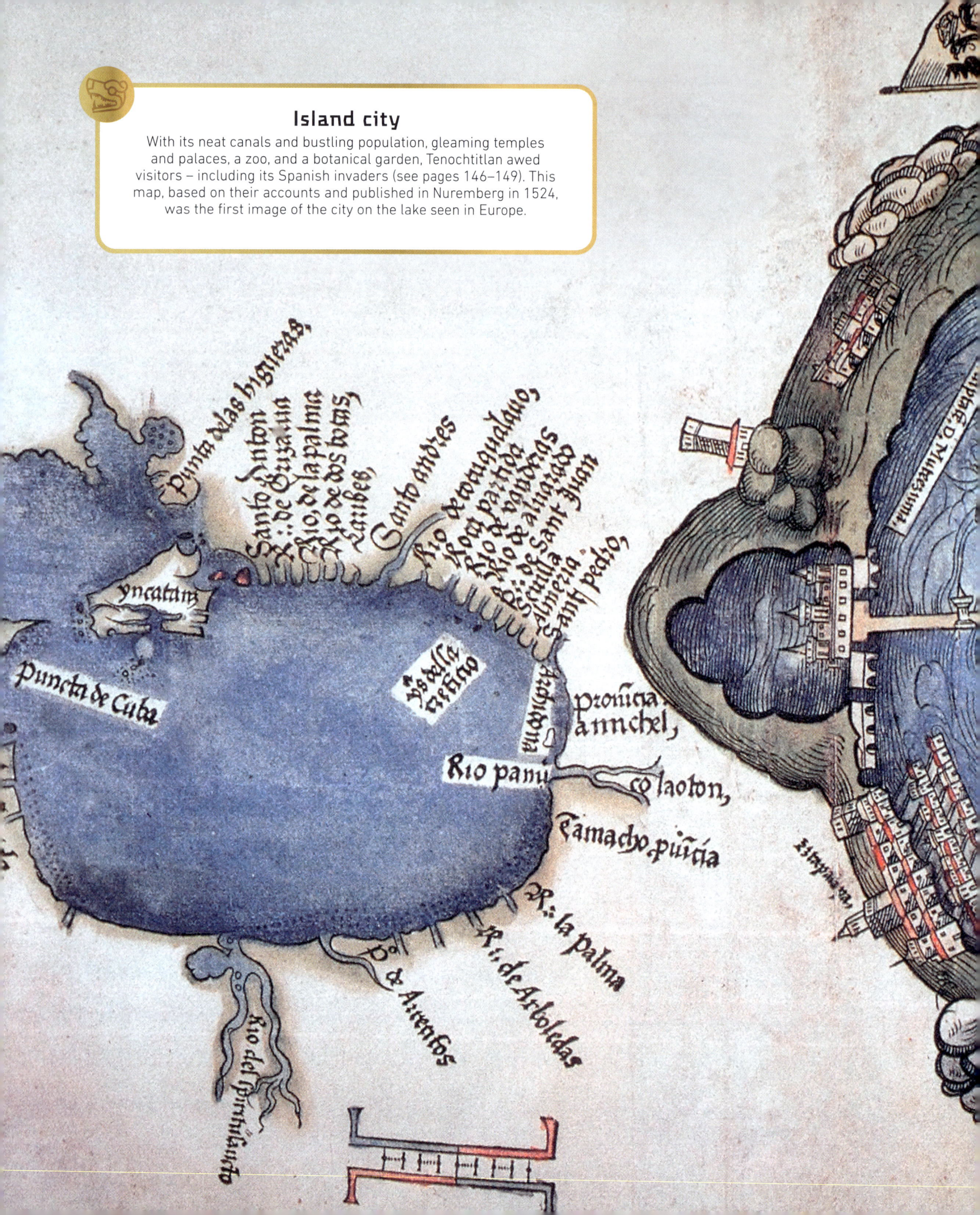

Island city

With its neat canals and bustling population, gleaming temples and palaces, a zoo, and a botanical garden, Tenochtitlan awed visitors – including its Spanish invaders (see pages 146–149). This map, based on their accounts and published in Nuremberg in 1524, was the first image of the city on the lake seen in Europe.

Life on the lake

The Aztecs depended on the water that surrounded them for food and keeping clean. By clever engineering, they dredged canals for transport and built long causeways to the mainland. Fresh water for drinking was piped in along aqueducts.

Houses usually had a thatched roof.

Canal-side living
Ordinary people lived in simple houses on the man-made islands surrounding the sacred centre of the city. Most had direct access to canals or lake water.

A woman weaving with her baby strapped to her back, while her daughter watches and learns

Man using a spear to catch food, perhaps hoping for a frog or an axolotl

Connected lakes

Tenochtitlan was located in a shallow part of the large, salty Lake Texcoco, which was linked to other lakes. To prevent flooding when water levels changed with the seasons, the Aztecs built a 16-km- (10-mile-) long dyke. This also kept an area of fresh water around the island, replenished with water from rivers and the lakes to the south.

KEY
- Saltwater
- Fresh water
- Causeway
- Dyke
- Chinampas (see pages 112–113)

Canoes for everything

Canoes carried people and cargo and were essential for fishermen. Larger canoes transported warriors to attack other lakeside towns.

Cargo
This young man is taking building materials to a temple. Canoes could handle heavy loads – even large stone statues.

Walking on water
Sturdy causeways led from Tenochtitlan to other cities along the shore. One carried fresh water from a mainland spring in an aqueduct. Wooden bridges allowed larger canoes through, and could be removed to stop enemies advancing.

Fishing
Fish and shellfish were caught from canoes to eat or sell at the market. This man is trapping a fish in his sack-shaped net.

- Nets placed in the canal to trap water birds
- Aqueduct
- Causeway
- Woman grinding maize for cooking
- Children cooling off during a break from doing chores

Ruler's transport
Moctezuma II travels across the water in a wide, steady canoe. It is large enough to carry his noble entourage, too.

Market day

The island city's biggest market was in adjoining Tlatelolco. Here, traders sold their wares on most days of the week. Each trader had their own space, and everything was strictly controlled.

① Snack vendors
Hungry market-goers can grab a tasty tamale, grilled corn on the cob, or a cake made of algae. Drinks include *atole*, a spiced cornmeal drink, served warm.

② Market inspector
An important official keeps an eye on everything, making sure trade rules are followed. His guards patrol the aisles, ready to step in if there's any trouble.

③ Kindling wood
People need plenty of sticks to light fires in the home for cooking and keeping warm. Priests buy bundles of them for temples, where they keep ceremonial fires going.

⑦ Holy smoke
Braziers and incense burners come in all shapes and sizes. Some feature gods, such as Tlaloc. They are used to burn copal resin as incense in homes, temples, and palaces.

⑧ Patterned cloth
Beautiful fabrics for capes and tunic-like blouses (*huipilli*) are on offer in this area. Some are woven locally, others have patterns typical of weavers from further afield.

⑨ Home storage
Clay pots and vessels are practical for storing anything from dried maize and beans to personal treasures. Some are used for cooking, or fetching water.

Market town

Tlatelolco was built by people who broke away from Tenochtitlan soon after the city's founding. It had its own temples next to the market. In 1473, it was conquered and incorporated into the main city, and its walled market square catered to around 30,000 buyers and sellers every day.

④ Maguey mat
Porters are moving heavy rolls of maguey-fibre mat. A shopper wonders how much of the matting she will need to cover the floor in her house.

⑤ Fruit and vegetables
Maize of all hues, squash, beans, tomatoes, hot and sweet chillies, and fruits such as guava and pineapple are on offer. Flowers add scents to the colourful displays.

⑥ Seasoning salt
Salt is very valuable. The salt seller uses the fixed market system to carefully measure out quantities in bowl units. Most customers can only afford to buy the smallest unit.

⑩ Fresh fish
Different species of fish, and tiny freshwater crayfish too, come in daily from the surrounding lake. Like most goods, loads are delivered by canoe at the market's own dock.

⑪ Apprentice traders
Many vendors bring their children so they can learn the trade early. This child might take over the stall as soon as they are old enough.

Buying and selling

Merchants and traders came from far and wide to sell their goods, from live animals and luxury items to food and homewares. This market scene only shows a fraction of all the things customers could buy.

Trade and tribute

The people of Tenochtitlan enjoyed many materials and goods from outside the city. Some, reserved for rulers and priests, were tribute paid by other city-states, while others were sold by travelling merchants.

Luxury goods
Travelling merchants (see pages 90–91) sold precious items in the market. These two sell jaguar pelts, ear spools, lip plugs, and necklaces.

Pelt of a jaguar

Conch pendant

Turquoise pendant with golden bells

Edible currency
Cacao beans, from the tropical Maya regions to the southeast, were used as money, as well as to make drinks.

Cacao beans

Coastal conches
Conch shells came from coastal communities far from Tenochtitlan. Large ones were used as trumpets and as offerings, while smaller shells decorated clothes or were made into earrings.

Mixtec skills
This pendant was crafted by a Mixtec goldsmith (see page 16). The turquoise in the centre came from a region to the northwest.

Conch-shell earrings

Brilliant birds
Feathers from many different birds were big business. Markets were also full of colourful living birds from tropical forests, such as the quetzal.

Quetzal bird with long tail feathers

Taxing tribute

Provinces controlled by the Aztecs had to pay a form of tax, called a tribute. This page from a codex (see page 152) lists how much of each item subject peoples were required to hand over every year.

1 x 20

20 x 20

400 x 20

Keeping count
Symbols showed the quantities required of each item. They were counted in units of 20. A flag meant 20, two flags meant 2 x 20, and so on. A feather was the sign for 20 x 20 (= 400). The bag meant 400 x 20 (= 8,000).

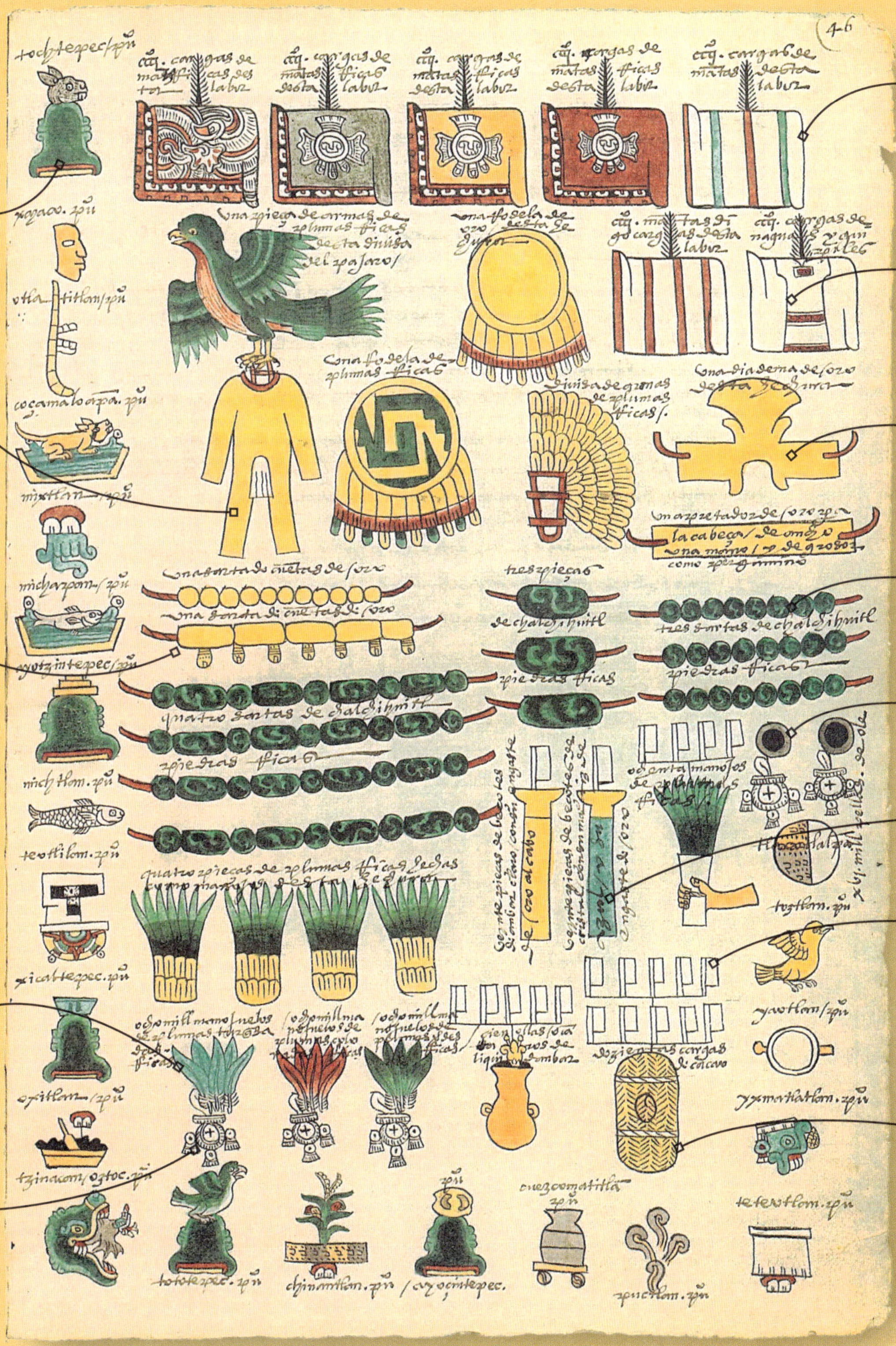

- Symbols for the towns that came together to pay this tribute are shown on the left side, starting with Tochtepec ("Rabbit Hill Place").
- A warrior costume, complete with shield and quetzal headdress
- Two necklaces made of gold beads, one of them with bells
- Bundles of bird feathers: blue cotinga, red spoonbill, and green quetzal
- The symbol of a bag (*xiquipilli*) here means a quantity of 8,000 of each feather colour.
- Cloaks woven in beautiful patterns, a speciality of the Tochtepec, with 2,400 of them to be supplied a year.
- 400 women's tunics and skirts
- One gold diadem
- Three necklaces with jade beads of different sizes
- 16,000 balls of rubber, for the ballgame
- Amber and crystal lip plugs, 20 of each set in gold
- Symbol of one flag shows a unit of 20. So here the quantity is 10 x 20 = 200 bags of cacao beans to be paid.
- 200 loads of cacao beans, packed in baskets

Daily life

Farming on the lake

When the Aztecs first settled on the island in Lake Texcoco, they did not have access to farmland on the shores. Instead, they reclaimed land from the lake itself, building islands known as *chinampas* to grow food on. People still farm on these today.

Cultivating crops
The *chinampas* were constructed in shallow waters. Fences contained the soil, and canoes passed along the canals between. Up to seven crops a year of maize, beans, squash, other vegetables, flowers, and herbs were grown in the rich, moist soil.

Willow and cypress trees at the edges hold the islands together.

Squash

Overseer in a cape

Tomatoes

Maguey-fibre bag

Flat-bottomed canoe

Amaranth flowers

Maize

Goose

Layering up

Up to around 200 m (650 ft) long and usually no more than 10 m (32 ft) wide, the *chinampas* were made by staking out the shallow lake bed and enclosing areas with a wattle fence. Layers of lake sediment and plant matter, dredged from the bottom of the lake by people in canoes, were added to the fence-lined area.

- Rich organic matter from the bottom of the lake is used as fertilizer.
- Wattle fence of woven willow and reeds
- Soil is kept moist by water from the lake and canals.
- Maize plants
- Sediment and mud are used to build up the *chinampa*.
- Cypress and willow tree roots hold the island together.

Great blue heron

Great white heron

Man prepares soil with a digging stick.

Reed basket

Beans

Heron

Woman sorts chillies.

Chilli peppers

Farmer hoeing weeds.

Top of the crops

The Aztecs farmed a wide variety of crops for food, medicine, and other uses. Many foods enjoyed worldwide today are native to the Americas and were unknown to Europeans before the Spanish invasion.

Petal passion
Flowers symbolized life's beauty and pleasures. Poets wrote about them and nobles wore them! Gardeners cultivated flowers to eat, as remedies, and for decoration and their scent — including developing most known varieties of marigold.

Fresh produce
The fruits, vegetables, and seeds illustrated here were all introduced to Europeans by the Aztecs. In some cases, the English name for them comes directly from Nahuatl (the Aztec language).

Squash (*ayotli*)
The Aztecs grew a variety of squashes. They ate the flesh and seeds, and used the dried-out skins as containers.

Chillies (*chilli*)
Chillies were an essential flavouring in food and drinks, adding spice. They were eaten fresh, cooked, or dried.

Tomatoes (*xitomatl*)
Aztec tomatoes were smaller than modern varieties — more like today's cherry tomatoes — and grew in shades of red, yellow, or purple.

Beans (*etl*)
Beans, of which there were several kinds, were a staple of the Aztec diet, providing vital protein at every meal.

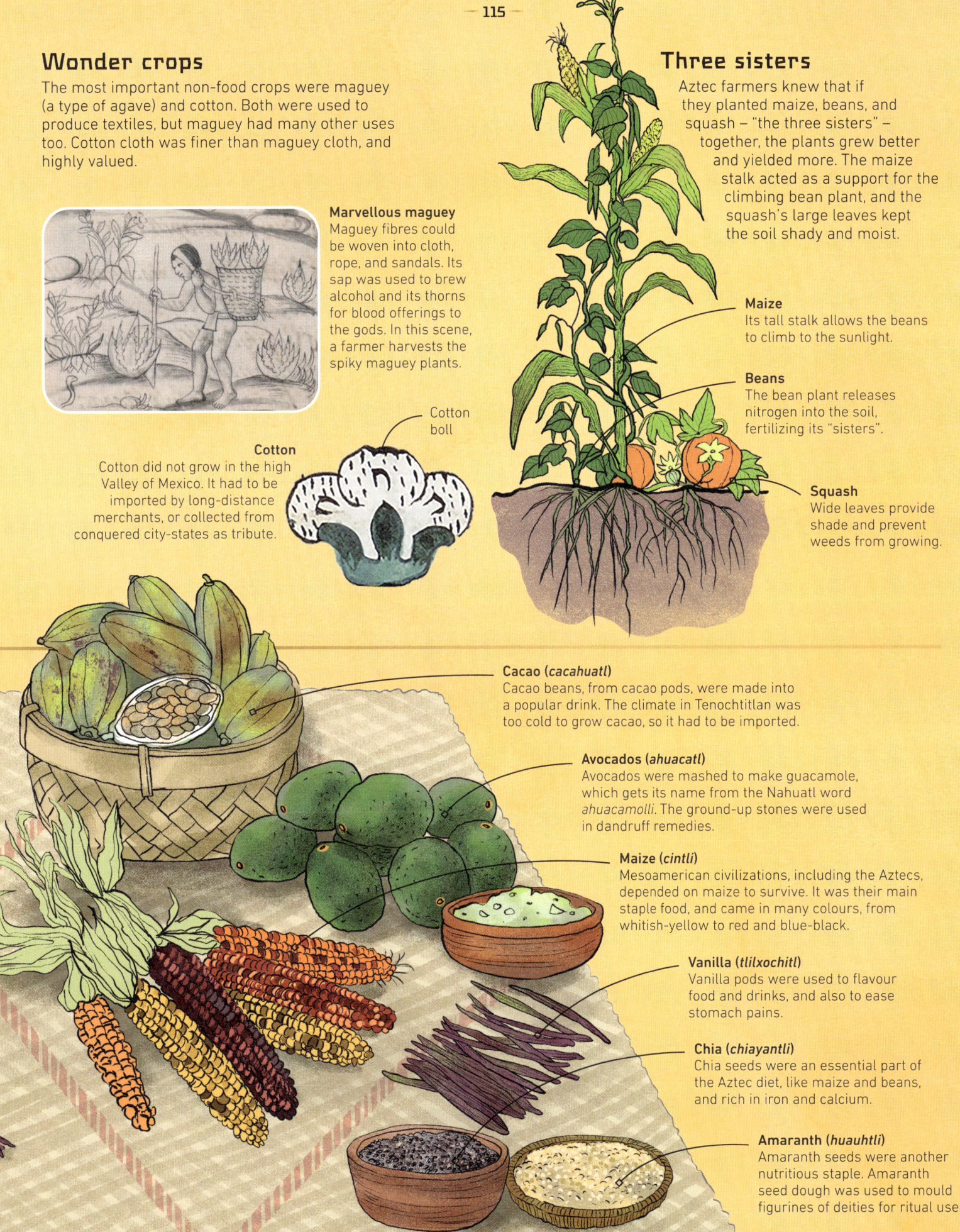

Wonder crops

The most important non-food crops were maguey (a type of agave) and cotton. Both were used to produce textiles, but maguey had many other uses too. Cotton cloth was finer than maguey cloth, and highly valued.

Marvellous maguey
Maguey fibres could be woven into cloth, rope, and sandals. Its sap was used to brew alcohol and its thorns for blood offerings to the gods. In this scene, a farmer harvests the spiky maguey plants.

Cotton boll

Cotton
Cotton did not grow in the high Valley of Mexico. It had to be imported by long-distance merchants, or collected from conquered city-states as tribute.

Three sisters

Aztec farmers knew that if they planted maize, beans, and squash – "the three sisters" – together, the plants grew better and yielded more. The maize stalk acted as a support for the climbing bean plant, and the squash's large leaves kept the soil shady and moist.

Maize
Its tall stalk allows the beans to climb to the sunlight.

Beans
The bean plant releases nitrogen into the soil, fertilizing its "sisters".

Squash
Wide leaves provide shade and prevent weeds from growing.

Cacao (*cacahuatl*)
Cacao beans, from cacao pods, were made into a popular drink. The climate in Tenochtitlan was too cold to grow cacao, so it had to be imported.

Avocados (*ahuacatl*)
Avocados were mashed to make guacamole, which gets its name from the Nahuatl word *ahuacamolli*. The ground-up stones were used in dandruff remedies.

Maize (*cintli*)
Mesoamerican civilizations, including the Aztecs, depended on maize to survive. It was their main staple food, and came in many colours, from whitish-yellow to red and blue-black.

Vanilla (*tlilxochitl*)
Vanilla pods were used to flavour food and drinks, and also to ease stomach pains.

Chia (*chiayantli*)
Chia seeds were an essential part of the Aztec diet, like maize and beans, and rich in iron and calcium.

Amaranth (*huauhtli*)
Amaranth seeds were another nutritious staple. Amaranth seed dough was used to mould figurines of deities for ritual use.

Kernels of life

In Aztec mythology, the creator god, Quetzalcoatl, gave maize to humans to keep them alive. The Aztecs celebrated the maize farming cycle (shown here) with seasonal festivals, honouring the deities that made the maize flourish with feasts held in many *veintenas* (20-day calendar periods).

Etzalcualiztli

In the sixth *veintena*, Etzalcualiztli, people celebrated the arrival of the rains. They feasted on maize and bean stew, and made offerings to the rain god Tlaloc in the hope of a good harvest.

- Tlaloc wears a necklace made of red and white maize ears.

- The planting cycle begins when the soil warms up enough to be tilled and the seeds can be sown.
- Maize sprouts young shoots.

Dry season (*tonalco*) | **Wet season (*xopan*)**

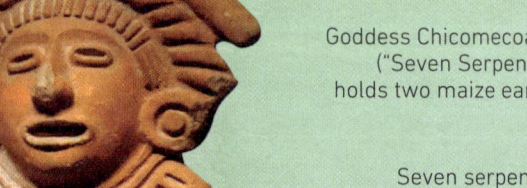

- Goddess Chicomecoatl ("Seven Serpent") holds two maize ears.
- Seven serpents symbolize the maize roots and her name.

Tititl

In Tititl, the 17th *veintena*, people celebrated the end of the winter frosts, when the soil warmed up and made it safe to plant again. They gathered the maize seeds stored from the previous harvest, and worshipped the fertility goddess Cihuacoatl ("Woman Snake").

Huey Tozoztli

The festival of Huey Tozoztli, in the fourth *veintena*, honoured two maize deities: Cinteotl and Chicomecoatl. The people took the best seeds to Chicomecoatl's temple, and asked her to bless them ready for sowing. They also prayed to the god Tlaloc for rain.

- People bring offerings of food, including chillies, to the goddess.

Cinteotl and Chicomecoatl

This god and goddess were associated with ripe maize as a life-giving food. They received prayers and offerings as the maize matured to ensure a plentiful harvest that would replenish the city's stores.

The figure of Cinteotl is made of a green stone that symbolizes fertility.

Chicomecoatl wears a tall "paper house" headdress and carries ripe ears of maize.

Ochpaniztli

The feast of Ochpaniztli, the 11th *veintena*, marked the end of harvest time and the return of the dry season. Now, the people begged Tlaloc not to send rain, so that the maize could be gathered and stored without being spoiled.

This priest, impersonating Tlaloc, carries a serpent staff.

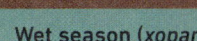

Wet season (*xopan*) — Dry season (*tonalco*)

Huey Tecuilhuitl

By the eighth *veintena*, food stores were low, and the lords gave out food to the poor. When the first green ears of maize appeared, the people worshipped Xilonen, goddess of young maize, and had their first taste of the new season's crop.

The goddess Xilonen carries young ears of maize in her left hand and a bone rattle staff, used in fertility rituals, in her right hand.

Itztlacoliuhqui

With the dry season came the danger of frosts, brought by the god Itztlacoliuhqui (above). There could be no planting until Tititl, when the cycle began again.

Favourite flavours

The Aztec diet was dominated by maize, vegetables, and fruit, but people also hunted or foraged for fish, meat, insects, and other wild foods, and relished luxuries such as cacao when they could get them.

Maize three ways
The Aztecs ate maize in many ways – even as popcorn! Most popular were tamales and tortillas – still eaten across Mexico today. Both are crafted from a dough made by soaking maize kernels in a mixture of water and ash, which softens them and releases their nutrients.

Tamales
These round parcels of dough were stuffed and then wrapped in maize leaves and steamed. Everyone ate them, especially at feasts, filled with beans, greens, eggs, or meat.

Pulque, an alcoholic drink made from maguey sap, was served too.

Baskets of tamales prepared for a feast

Popcorn
The rock-hard kernels of maize grown by the Aztecs were perfect for popping.

Tortillas
These plain, round flatbreads were made from dough and cooked on a clay plate. Teenage girls learned from their mothers how to prepare the dough using a grinding stone.

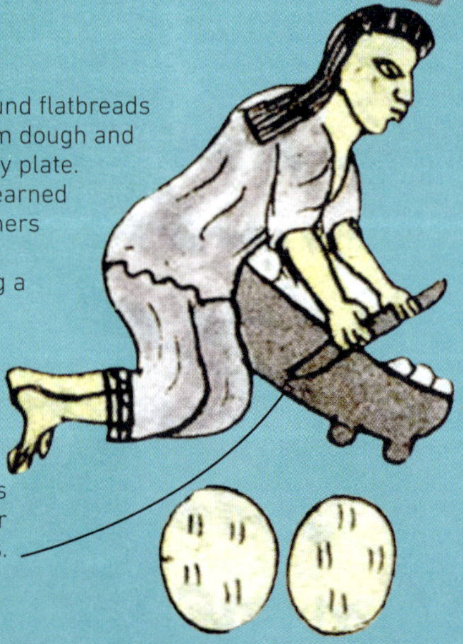

A girl grinds maize into flour to make tortillas.

> A number of women, maidens, danced... They danced the popcorn dance. As thick as tassels of maize were their popcorn garlands.
>
> Florentine Codex

Tasty treats

Although meals were based around maize, beans, and vegetables, people topped up their diet with some protein-rich treats. Spiced, toasted grasshoppers, for example, were a delicacy – and continue to be relished in modern Mexico.

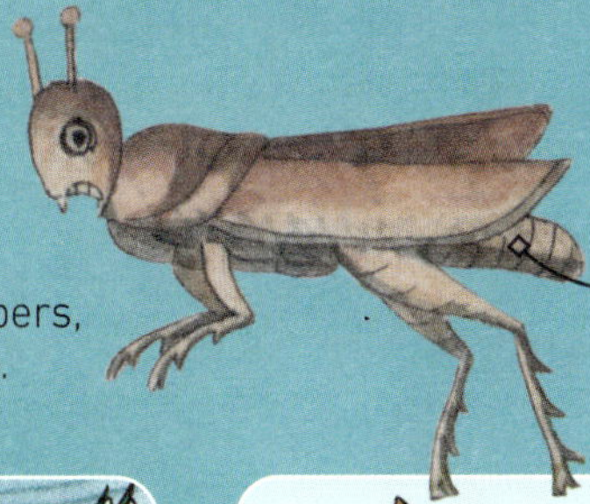

Crispy grasshoppers made a popular snack.

Algae
Blue-green algae grew on the surface of Lake Texcoco. Farmers skimmed it from the water, let it dry in the sun, and formed it into square cakes, which were rich in protein, vitamins, and minerals.

Water boatmen
The lake was full of these insects, which were trapped in nets and then ground into dough to make a type of tamale. The real treat, though, was their eggs, collected from floating grass traps.

Meaty treats
Although a few people kept turkeys, ducks, and dogs for meat, they were a luxury reserved for nobles and feast days. However, fish and wild fowl were available to those who could catch them.

Drinking chocolate

Among the nobles, *cacahuatl* was the drink of choice. Although it was made from cacao beans, from which we make chocolate today, it would have tasted very different! They flavoured the drink with sweet or spicy ingredients, including flowers, vanilla, and chillies.

Traded treasure
Traders travelled hundreds of miles to obtain cacao for the empire. This statue is thought to depict a merchant holding a cacao pod.

Custard-apple flower

Honey

Vanilla

Chillies

The art of foam
Making *cacahuatl* took skill and practice. It involved adding water to the ground beans, little by little, and then pouring the liquid back and forth between two containers, from a height, until it became smooth and foamy.

Herbal know-how

Aztec herbalists learned from experience how to prepare roots, leaves, and flowers to make the most of their health benefits, recording their herbal remedies in illustrated books. Some remedies needed a touch of magic, too.

Fever
To bring down a fever, the patient drank a series of infusions, made by steeping the roots of certain herbs and a type of tomato in water.

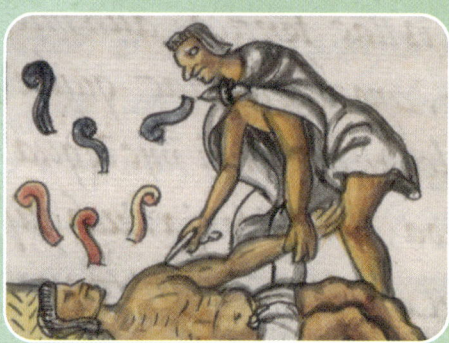

Snake bite
First the bite was sucked, before making cuts to the swollen area and wrapping it in maguey-fibre cloth. Both patient and healer also prayed to the relevant gods.

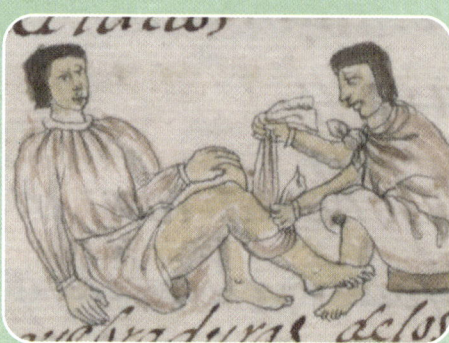

Fractured leg
The wound was cleaned with warm, sterile urine and then treated with hot, antibacterial maguey sap. Surgeons inserted a wooden splint and set the leg in plant plaster.

Tooth care
To prevent plaque, people cleaned their teeth with ground charcoal, then rinsed their mouths with salt. They also applied a mixture of cochineal, chilli, and salt.

Trips and falls
People who suffered a fall were advised to drink hot urine mixed with ground-up lizards and a pinch of soot, followed by an infusion of acidic roots and herbs.

Lightning strike
Being struck by lightning was believed to cause confusion. Drinking cold water mixed with scrapings from a special stone restored a person to their senses.

Botanical garden

In 1467, Moctezuma I created what was perhaps the world's first botanical garden, planted with medicinal plants from across the empire. Healers and patients were encouraged to experiment with them.

Tlatlacotic
Root taken to relieve chest pain related to anxiety

Quetzalatzoyatl, Acocotli, and Tetzitzilin
Used to treat epileptic seizures

Quauhtlaxoxocoyolin
Believed to prevent hair loss and dandruff

Healing and herbs

Expert plant knowledge, experience of war surgery, and high standards of cleanliness – plus a helping hand from the gods – enabled Aztec healers to treat a variety of health problems.

Gods of healing

The Aztecs worshipped several deities believed to have the power to both cause and cure diseases. One was Ixtlilton ("Small Black Face"), a gentle god who brought sick children healing darkness, warding off nightmares and letting them recover with peaceful sleep.

Ixtlilton is shown wearing a black mask, symbolizing the healing power of darkness.

This man can be seen talking to a village healer about a problem.

The healer, like many, is a woman.

The healer throws maize kernels while praying to the god Ehecatl–Quetzalcoatl.

Community healers

Healers were understood to have a special ability to diagnose illnesses. They identified a problem's cause by throwing maize kernels and "reading" how they fell – a practice used by village healers in Mexico even today.

Huitzitzilixochitl
Used to treat patients suffering from fatigue

Teonochtli and Teoiztaquilitl
Prescribed to soothe toothache and sore throats

Ayauhquahuitl and Quauhiyauhtli
Used to counter lightning strikes

Tepepapaloquilitl
Believed to help in safely crossing a river

Clean living

Keeping clean was vital to both physical and spiritual health. By keeping body, soul, and the city around them in good order, the Aztecs kept their world in balance.

Bathing
Men and women of all classes washed themselves often in the lake and canals, rivers, and pools.

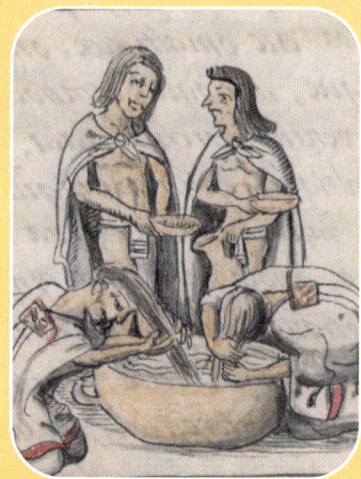

Hair washing
When a merchant went abroad, he and his family did not wash their hair until he was safely home.

Keeping clean
In the home, children learned from their parents the importance of washing themselves, wearing clean clothes, and sweeping away dirt. Outdoors, Tenochtitlan's streets were swept clean every day.

Xiuhamolli flowers

Xiuhamolli roots

Soap plant
The roots of the soapwort (*xiuhamolli*) plant produced a soapy lather suitable for cleaning bodies, hair, and clothes. Some *xiuhamolli* flowers were used dye hair gold.

A healthy sweat
As well as bathing outdoors, people enjoyed going to a steam room, used for cleansing, relaxation, health treatments, and to support childbirth. One of the walls was heated by an external furnace and water was thrown at it to make steam.

- Image of the fertility goddess Tlazolteotl
- A man awaits his turn.
- The doorway of the steam room was low and small to keep heat in.
- A domed structure contains a roaring fire.
- A healer offers a medicinal drink to a weeping man.
- A woman feeds the fire with more wood.

Birth preparations
In the steam room, a midwife massages the mother-to-be's belly to relax her and position the baby for birth.

Bathing the newborn
Straight after the birth, the midwife shows the new mother how to bathe her newborn baby.

Praying for purity
The midwife sings to Chalchiuhtlicue, goddess of water and fertility, to purify the baby's heart.

Steam birth
The steam room had special importance as a place where midwives and women came before, during, and after childbirth – an experience the Aztecs saw as a kind of battle.

> And when the baby had arrived on Earth, then the midwife shouted; she gave war cries, which meant that the little woman had fought a good battle, had become a brave warrior, had taken a captive, had captured a baby.
>
> Florentine Codex

Skull-faced heroines
Women who died in childbirth were regarded as brave heroines, like fallen warriors. However, some were thought to return to Earth as a kind of spirit with a skull-like face.

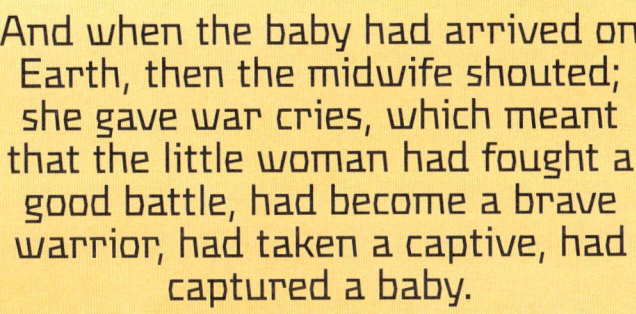

This female figure represents a woman giving birth.

Filth goddess Tlazolteotl
As a fertility goddess with the power to eat dirt and cleanse human souls, Tlazolteotl was often honoured at the steam room.

Dress like an Aztec

Boys and men

Men, regardless of class, wore a loincloth (*maxtlatl*) and, if they had one, a cloak (*tilmatli*). It was the quality of the fabric and its decoration that indicated a person's status.

Young boy
Until they were teenagers, boys simply wore a short cloak tied at the shoulder.

Young boys wore no loincloth.

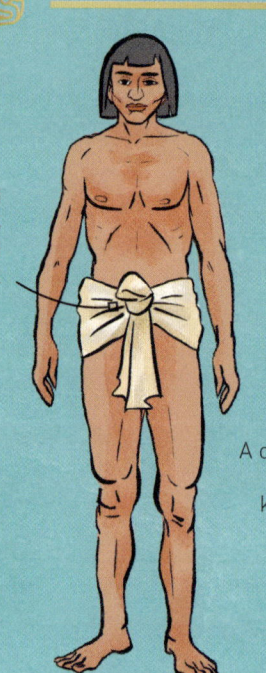

Fabric passed between the legs and tied around the waist.

Male commoner
Poorer adult commoners wore a plain loincloth woven from maguey fibre.

A commoner's cloak was knee-length.

Wealthier commoner
Commoners who could afford one wore an undecorated maguey-fibre cloak.

Girls and women

Women, who generally showed less skin than men, wore a tunic-like blouse (*huipilli*) over a simple skirt (*cueitl*). Like the men, commoner women dressed in maguey fibre, while noblewomen wore cotton.

Young girl
Very young girls wore a short, plain tunic-like blouse, without a skirt.

Skirts were tied around the waist by a sash, under the blouse.

Older girl
Girls that were older also wore a tunic-like blouse with a knee-length skirt underneath.

Maguey fibre had a coarser texture than cotton.

Tunic-like blouses could fall to hip level or below.

Female commoner
Adult commoner women wore an ankle-length skirt, paired with a plain blouse.

For an Aztec, knowing – and showing – their place in society was important. A person's clothes often revealed their age, social status, and occupation.

The cape is woven from maguey fibre.

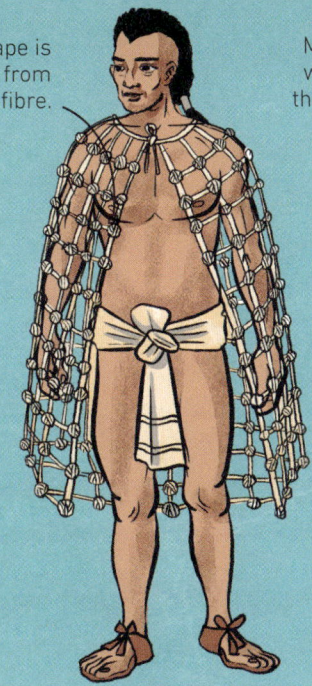

Most cloaks were tied at the shoulder.

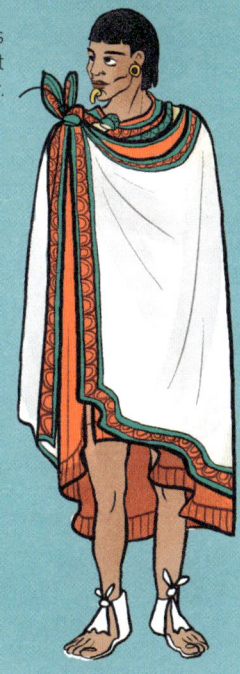

Jewellery was also a sign of rank.

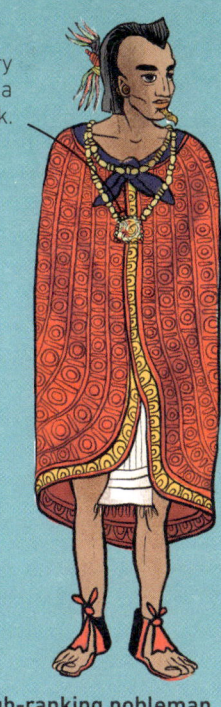

Male merchant
Merchants, often wealthier than other commoners, might wear a patterned cloak.

Schoolteacher
A knee-length net cape was sometimes worn by schoolteachers.

Male noble
Wearing one cotton cloak over another signified wealth and status, and provided warmth.

High-ranking nobleman
A few top nobles knotted their cloak at the front to display their status.

Quechquemitl, made of two rectangular pieces of cloth joined to make a triangular shape, with tassels

Noblewomen enhanced their outfits with precious beads.

Yellow face paint symbolized maturity.

Sandals were typically a sign of high status.

Female merchant
A wealthy merchant still had to wear maguey fibre, but could afford a decorative blouse.

Noblewoman in *quechquemitl*
Some noblewomen wore this garment and goddesses are often depicted wearing one.

Noblewoman
A colourful cotton blouse with an elaborate border signified a woman's noble status.

High-ranking noblewoman
Women with royal connections might wear embroidered cotton, trimmed with rabbit fur.

Tubular ear spools
These are made of polished obsidian and crystal.

Gold nose ornament
Nose plugs such as this one were associated with deities.

Round ear spools
This fine pottery spool has a flower motif.

Some women painted their face yellow to show maturity.

Greenstone and shell necklace
Shell and greenstone were both linked with fertility.

Eagle lip plug
Gold lip plugs were awarded to top warriors.

Conch shell pendant
This "wind jewel" carved like a feathered serpent recalls the wind god Ehecatl-Quetzalcoatl.

Jewellery for the nobles
Both men and women wore jewellery, though men wore more. While commoners had beads of polished stone and bone, nobles were permitted to wear rarer materials, such as greenstone, obsidian, shell, and gold.

Shell bracelet
Red spondylus shell, from the Pacific Ocean, was prized for its colour.

Dressing up

As everyone wore similar types of garments, people relied on colour and ornament to make their outfits special. Those who were entitled to, embellished their clothes with vivid designs and embroidery, and added jewellery.

A noblewoman's blouse

No complete items of Aztec clothing survive today, but this modern *huipilli* – a kind of tunic-like blouse – woven by a Maya artisan is similar to the ones worn by Aztec noblewomen.

Intricate geometric or floral patterns were woven into or embroidered onto the material.

The triangular shapes around the neckline resemble the Sun's rays.

Four rosettes, on the front, back, and shoulders, represent the cardinal points.

The main colours, made from natural dyes, were reds, yellows, blacks, and blues. The illustrations below show how some of these dyes were made.

The *huipilli* is made of several panels of woven white cotton cloth, stitched together.

Red
Cochineal, a bright red dye, was made by drying and crushing tiny red insects into a powder, and adding water.

Yellow
Various flowers were picked and crushed to make yellow. The name of this one, *xochipalli*, means "flower paint".

Black
Splitting and then soaking the tough bark of the logwood tree produced a dark reddish-black dye.

Indigo
Dark blue was obtained by pounding and squeezing the juice from a plant identified today as wild indigo.

Aztec hairdos

In the Aztec world, no one cut or arranged their hair on a whim. Hair had many cultural and religious meanings, and every age and stage of life, as well as a person's status, was characterized by a certain hairdo.

Looking the part

Boys and men were expected to cut and style their hair in a particular way, depending on their occupation – from a simple commoners' crop to symbolic up-dos.

Young boy
Hair was associated with maturity, so boys had their heads shaved until they were 10 years old, then cut short.

Long tuft of hair worn by youth who has not yet taken a captive

Youth
From age 10, boys allowed a tuft of hair to grow at the nape of their neck. This was cut when a youth took his first captive.

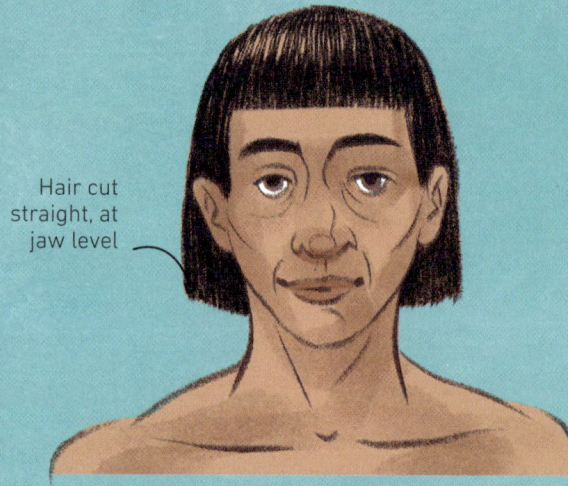

Hair cut straight, at jaw level

Adult man
Cutting off the tuft marked the switch to adulthood. Most men then grew and cut their hair into a bob style.

Red cord holds "pillar" in place.

Standard warrior
Lower-ranking warriors were entitled to tie their hair with a red cord into a pillar-like topknot called a *temillotl*.

Masses of hair provide spiritual protection.

Priest
Priests never washed, combed, or cut their hair, wearing it long and matted to stop their spiritual energy (*tonalli*) escaping.

Patch of hair over the ear

Elite warrior
Top-ranking *cuachic* ("shorn") warriors shaved most of their hair, leaving a ridge in the middle and a long section at the back.

Seizing an enemy's hair symbolized his surrender.

Significant hair

The Aztecs believed hair protected the head, stopping their spiritual energy (*tonalli*) from escaping. When a warrior took a captive, he gripped his hair and cut it off as a trophy, taking away the enemy's spirit and honour.

> The captors took hair from the crowns of the captives' heads... Thus it was shown that he was indeed a taker of captives.
>
> Florentine Codex

The ends of each twist stick up, like horns.

Women's styles

Girls wore their hair down, but once married, women usually kept their long hair neatly tied up. Pictures of Aztec women suggest that most wore very similar up-dos, sometimes adding natural dyes for shine and a hint of colour.

Unmarried girl
Girls' hair was cut short until they were about 12 years old. Once it grew, they wore it long and loose until they were married.

Married woman
Most married women divided their hair into two twists, brought around each side of the head, and secured near the forehead.

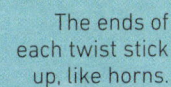

Female temple workers sometimes tinted their hair red.

Crossover style
Other styles included a variation on the classic married up-do, with the two horn-like ends crossed over at the front.

Bun style
Here, the hair is parted down the middle and coiled into two buns on either side of the head.

Colour and shine
Dyeing the hair with indigo, made from flowers, gave it a blue-black tone and a glossy sheen.

Precious plumage

Exotic feathers in shimmering colours were the Aztecs' most cherished valuables. Above all, they prized the green feathers of the quetzal bird, from tropical Central America.

Sacred beauty
The Aztecs thought of feathers as shining jewels, fit for the gods. Wearing feathers brought the wearer closer to the gods.

The headdress is made of around 12,000 feathers.

There were more than 1,500 gold ornaments

Some 450 quetzal tail feathers fan out around the headdress.

"Moctezuma's" headdress
Aztec feather workers crafted many headdresses, but only this one survives. Made of dazzling green, blue, and red feathers, it has become known as "Moctezuma's" headdress, although it probably never belonged to the ruler.

The blue feathers come from the blue cotinga bird and the deep-red feathers from red spoonbills.

Statement shields

As a reward for success on the battlefield, warriors received fine shields decorated with intricate feather designs. It is thought the animal on this shield, highlighted in blue cotinga feathers and gold sheet, may represent a warrior in a coyote costume.

Feather tassels hang from the shield's lower edge.

Water and fire, symbolizing war, pour from the creature's mouth.

Art of the feather

Specialized artisans working with feathers were called *amantecatl*. The Florentine Codex describes and illustrates featherworkers creating various intricate adornments.

Making banners and fans
When making fans, banners, and back ornaments, featherworkers usually tied the feathers to a wooden frame.

Fantastic fans

Feather fans were carried in ritual dances and by warriors and envoys as symbols of high rank. This one was found near the site of Tenochtitlan's Great Temple.

The feathers came from hummingbirds and parakeets.

Making shields
Shield-making involved trimming and fixing the feathers to a cloth base using glue made from orchid bulbs.

A symbol of power
The size and splendour of the headdress suggest it was made for a ruler or mighty warrior.

The feathers would have shimmered as the wearer moved.

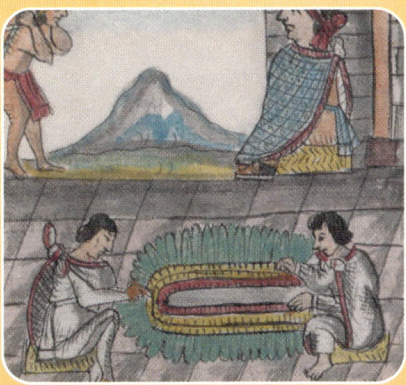

Making headdresses
Headdress-makers used a combination of glue and cord to attach the feathers to a flexible, netted frame.

Polished treasures

The Aztecs prized certain shells and stones, especially greenstone and turquoise. They polished these until they gleamed and wore them as status symbols.

Greenstone

Green-coloured stones symbolized fertility, life, and renewal. Of these, jadeite was the rarest and most valuable, coming from a Maya area in what is now Guatemala.

Skeletal deity
This delicately carved greenstone figure is thought to have been used as an incense container during ceremonies.

Jadeite necklace
Wearing strings of polished jadeite beads like these was a privilege reserved for nobles and deities.

Conch-shaped pendant
Impersonators of the god Ehecatl-Quetzalcoatl, whose symbol was a conch, may have worn this jadeite and gold pendant.

Obsidian

Obsidian is a type of hard volcanic glass created by rapidly cooling lava. When polished, it is both transparent and reflective, and was used to make mirrors, jewellery, and knives.

Looking glass
Soothsayers used obsidian mirrors to see into other worlds and communicate with ancestors and deities.

Cutting-edge blade
Obsidian was shaped into razor-sharp blades to make objects including surgical tools, weapons, and knives for ritual sacrifice.

Head of Xochipilli
This sculpted obsidian head depicts the god Xochipilli ("Flower Prince"), who was associated with noble pleasures, beauty, and love.

Tricolour lip plug
A labret signalled that the wearer's words and breath were precious. This one combines shell, red obsidian, and turquoise.

Turquoise

Turquoise reminded the Aztecs of life-giving water and fire. It came from distant lands – southern Mexico or what is now the American southwest – and from it they created exquisite mosaics and jewellery.

Mosaic mask
This mask, dotted with knobbly turquoise "spots", may represent Nanahuatzin ("Pimply Faced"), who became the Fifth Sun.

Sacrificial knife
This knife handle, inlaid with turquoise, malachite, and shells, is shaped like an eagle warrior.

Wind jewel
Priests serving the god Ehecatl-Quetzalcoatl, Lord of the Winds, wore his symbol: a cut-through conch shell.

Sea-snail pectoral
This intricate shell chest ornament was carved by the Huaxtecs, a Gulf Coast people, who were conquered by the Aztecs and paid tribute to them.

Shell

The Aztecs treasured shiny shells, which they associated with gods of war, water, and fertility. Pearl oyster and red spondylus came from the Pacific coast, and conch from the Gulf of Mexico.

Mother-of-pearl fish
These fish pendants, shaped from shimmering mother-of-pearl and symbolizing water's life-giving power, may have been strung together on a necklace.

Gift of the gods

The Aztecs called gold the "excrement of the gods". They prized the metal – although for them it was less precious than exotic feathers – using it to make exquisite items for rulers and nobles. Later, the Spanish melted many of these down.

Embossed animal heads run around the outer band.

Bands of jadeite mosaics made this disc even more precious.

Gold and jadeite disc
This disc, made of a sheet of embossed gold on wood, was crafted by skilled Mixtec goldsmiths, from a region conquered by the Aztecs. It may have been delivered to the ruler as tribute.

Serrated fangs and teeth add to impact.

Serpent lip plug
This sinuous gold serpent's head lip plug, with its powerful jaw, was designed to show off the power and status of its wearer.

Tongue moves to impress onlookers.

Lip plug was worn in pierced lower lip.

Feather plumage is crafted from gold strands.

The warrior holds darts and a shield in his left hand.

Eagle warrior bell
This warrior wears an eagle helmet and feathered headdress, and his bell-shaped body is decorated with feathers.

Bared teeth give a menacing impression.

Bell pendant
This cast-gold head has the features of a high-ranking warrior and is designed to intimidate enemies. It is a bell and has a loop so it can be worn as a pendant.

Snake-headed spear-thrower

A heron-feather plume suggests this is a warrior god.

Eagle ear ornaments
This pair of exquisitely crafted ear ornaments would have rattled and chimed in motion.

The warrior holds two darts, a banner, and a shield in his left hand.

Warrior figurine
This elite warrior figure has an Aztec-style face, dress, and trappings. He wears sandals, a loin cloth and belt with bells on it, ear spools, and a lip plug befitting his status.

Finely crafted feather plumes on the head

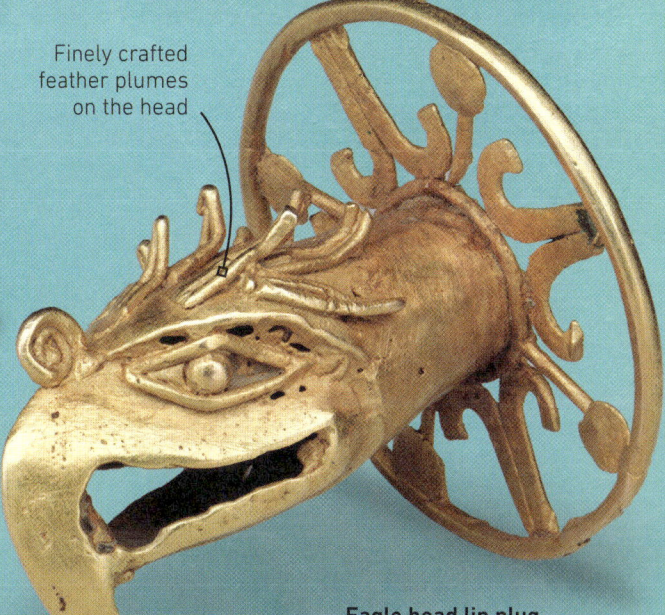

Eagle head lip plug
This lip plug takes the form of an eagle ready to attack its prey. It would have been worn by a high-ranking warrior.

Writing in pictures

Red lines show the reading direction, here vertically up and down from bottom right.

Fold-out books
Unlike European books, with pages bound along one side, the pages were attached in one long strip, which folded like a screen. This rare pre-colonial Mixtec screenfold book is a record of the rulers of the city-state of Tilantongo.

Figures are painted in red, black, yellow, and blue on deerskin.

Scribes
Talented artists called scribes were able to paint scenes and symbols. They used feather brushes and coloured inks made from plants and minerals to paint on tree bark paper or animal skins.

Storytelling
Some books were designed to be read aloud to an audience. A storyteller used the pictures as prompts, adding song and details as they performed.

What's in a name?
Scribes recorded place names using glyphs. These were figures or characters that combined pictograms (drawings representing an element of the name) with symbols indicating how the name sounded. Here are two decoded Nahuatl place glyphs. The ending "co" was often added to make it clear the name referred to a place – as in "Totoltzinco", right.

Place name		Pictogram		Sound symbol
	=		+	
Mazatlan Together, these glyphs mean "Deer Place".		*mazatl* (deer) A deer's head represents the Nahuatl for deer, "*mazatl*".		*tlantli* (teeth) Teeth show the name contains the sound "*tlan*", meaning "place".
	=		+	
Totoltzinco This glyph combination means "Little Turkey Place".		*totolin* (turkey) A turkey's head shows the name includes "*totol*".		*tzintli* (bottom) The word for bottom sounds like "*tzin*", also meaning "little".

The Aztecs recorded their history, myths, and religious calendars and rituals in books. Their spoken language, Nahuatl, was originally presented in pictures, not words.

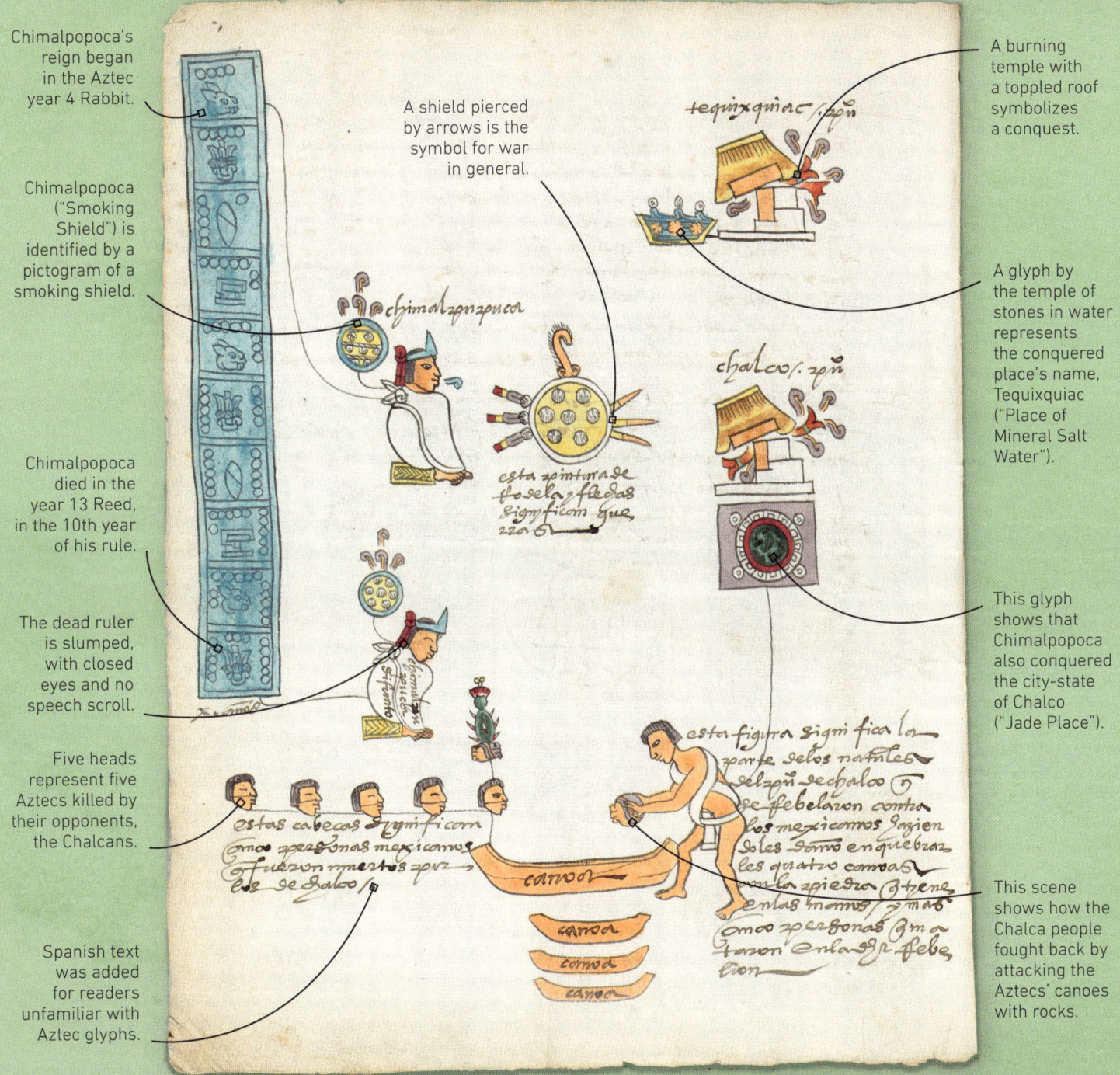

- Chimalpopoca's reign began in the Aztec year 4 Rabbit.
- Chimalpopoca ("Smoking Shield") is identified by a pictogram of a smoking shield.
- Chimalpopoca died in the year 13 Reed, in the 10th year of his rule.
- The dead ruler is slumped, with closed eyes and no speech scroll.
- Five heads represent five Aztecs killed by their opponents, the Chalcans.
- Spanish text was added for readers unfamiliar with Aztec glyphs.
- A shield pierced by arrows is the symbol for war in general.
- A burning temple with a toppled roof symbolizes a conquest.
- A glyph by the temple of stones in water represents the conquered place's name, Tequixquiac ("Place of Mineral Salt Water").
- This glyph shows that Chimalpopoca also conquered the city-state of Chalco ("Jade Place").
- This scene shows how the Chalca people fought back by attacking the Aztecs' canoes with rocks.

A ruler's reign in pictures

This page from the Codex Mendoza, an Aztec history book written by Nahua scribes shortly after the Spanish invasion, illustrates key events in the reign of the third Aztec ruler, Chimalpopoca. It uses pictograms to represent events and ideas.

Book of the days

Each page of the Aubin Tonalamatl charts one 13-day period (*trecena*) in the ritual calendar. Here, the rain god Tlaloc, chief deity of the seventh *trecena*, appears with the maize goddess Chicomecoatl in the large rectangle. The squares represent the day signs and the deities that influence them. More than 5 m (18 ft) long, this 16th-century screenfold book is read from right to left.

The House of Song

Young men gathered at the House of Song (*cuicacalli*) to sing and play music. Jaguar and eagle warriors, especially, rehearsed chants and dances there to perform during public ceremonies.

Youth band
This painting depicts young warriors at the House of Song, singing, playing, and dancing to the rhythm of drums.

Flutes
Made of reed, bone, or pottery, flutes were played at festivals honouring the god Tezcatlipoca.

Huehuetl
This vertical drum carved with symbols of war, including eagles and jaguars, and topped with animal skin, was played with the hands.

Dried seed pods and gourds were used as rattles.

Whistle
Pottery whistles were used for worship at home and in temples, and to sound signals in battle.

Teponaztli
This horizontal carved wooden drum was beaten with rubber-tipped sticks and could produce two tones.

The art of song

Music had sacred significance, playing an essential part in people's lives, whether they were rich or poor. The Nahuatl word for "music" is *cuicatlamatiliztli* – "the art of song".

Songs for the gods
Playing music was a way of worshipping the gods. During religious ceremonies, the sound of drums, rattles, and chanting filled the air.

A sculpture of Xochipilli, god of music, poetry, and dancing

A colourfully dressed acrobat rolls a log with his feet, to the beat of drums.

Songs of the court
Music was also performed for pleasure. Professional musicians worked at the ruler's palace so they were always available to provide entertainment.

Flower songs
Poetry was recited at ceremonies and celebrations. Known as "flower and song", it was often accompanied by music.

Rattle
The rain-like clatter of rattles often accompanied rituals related to fertility, rain-making, and farming.

The ballgame

The Aztecs loved to play *ollamaliztli*, their version of the ballgame enjoyed by peoples across Mesoamerica since Olmec times. It was a favourite sport of the nobles, and an important fixture on feast days.

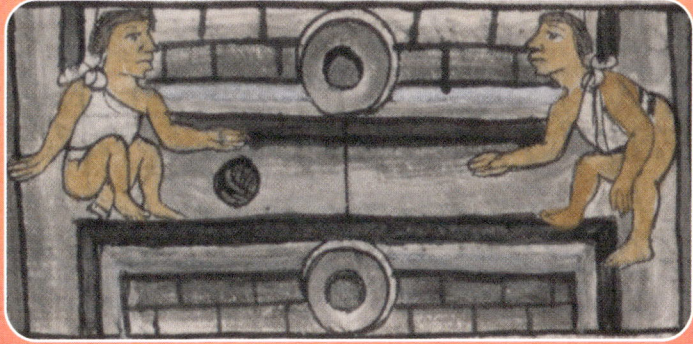

The ball court
This drawing of the Aztec ball court is not to scale, but shows the narrow, rectangular central section with cross sections at each end, lined by high walls, with a stone hoop on each of the side walls for scoring goals.

Getting the ball through a hoop meant victory.

Fancy feather cloaks were a luxury worth playing for.

High stakes
Players frequently gambled on the outcome of the game. Every type of valuable could be won or lost, from feather cloaks to gold jewellery, cacao, land, and even players' lives.

Rules of play
The rules of the game varied, but it was played by two teams of one or more players, who kept the ball in play using their hips, buttocks, or knees – never their hands or feet. Teams scored by getting the ball to the opposite end of the court, or through a hoop.

This bauble-like ball appears in a painting of a ballgame contest between gods.

Ball supplies
Rubber (*ollin*) for the balls came from an area on the Gulf of Mexico. The empire's demand for balls was so high that one province had to supply 16,000 balls each year as tribute.

End of an empire

Cortés leading his company

Spanish adventurers
In the name of their monarchs, lots of Spanish men set out to make their fortune in the Americas. In February 1519, a party led by Hernán Cortés landed on the coast of Mexico, and began to move inland. Some travelled on horseback, while Indigenous porters carried their supplies.

Heron, the bird glyph symbolizing Tlaxcalan warriors

Aztec adversaries
At this time, the Aztecs ruled or controlled most of the people living in the region. But one people, the Tlaxcala, who lived east of Lake Texcoco, never gave in to them. Hostile to the Spanish at first, they took the chance to defeat the Aztecs by becoming Spanish allies.

Hernán Cortés
Among the many who sought their luck in Mesoamerica was Hernán Cortés, a minor Spanish noble. After playing a part in the colonization of Cuba, he set out to conquer the mainland – disobeying the orders of his superior.

Arrival of the Spanish

In 1492, a Genoese navigator called Christopher Columbus sailed into the Caribbean on a voyage backed by Spain. Spanish interest in what they called the "New World" soon led sailors to Aztec lands in search of riches.

Moctezuma II

Ruler of the Aztec empire since 1503, and a trained priest and brave and successful warrior before that, Moctezuma was an experienced and powerful leader who controlled a large territory in the Valley of Mexico. To his people, he was also a representative of their god, Huitzilopochtli.

Malintzin

Born to a Nahua noble family, Malintzin was enslaved as a child and taken to live in a Maya town. When Cortés arrived, she was given to him. She spoke the languages of both the Aztecs and the Maya, and became a translator. All communication between Moctezuma and Cortés went through her. She was soon fluent in Spanish, too.

Interesting guests

Moctezuma II was expecting Cortés and was curious about the foreigners and their horses. Cortés had his eye on the Aztecs' wealth and land. In November 1519, Moctezuma allowed Cortés entry into Tenochtitlan, receiving him in his palace and offering him gifts.

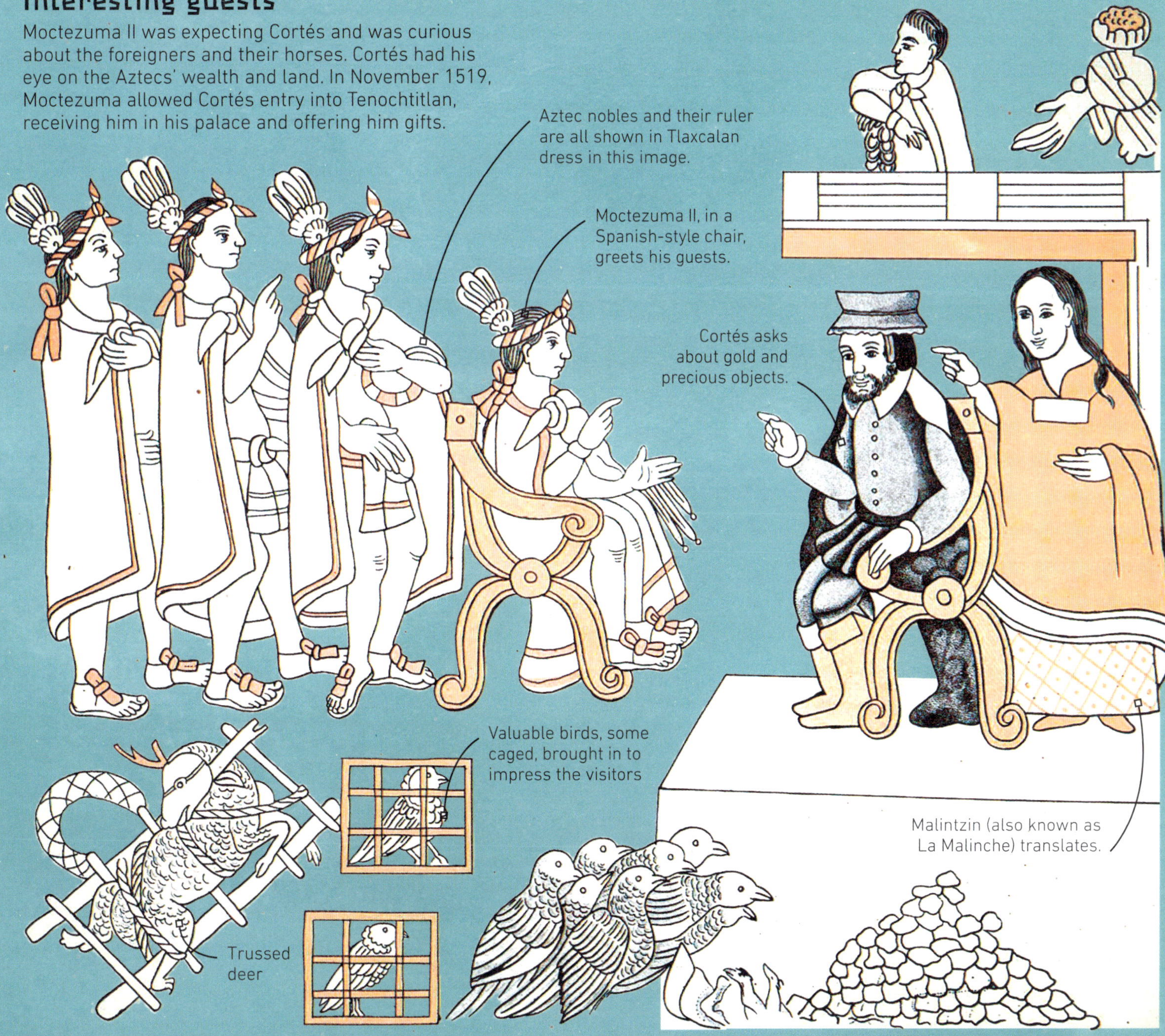

Aztec nobles and their ruler are all shown in Tlaxcalan dress in this image.

Moctezuma II, in a Spanish-style chair, greets his guests.

Cortés asks about gold and precious objects.

Valuable birds, some caged, brought in to impress the visitors

Malintzin (also known as La Malinche) translates.

Trussed deer

Defence and defeat

After the friendly start, relations between the Aztecs and Spanish soured. Tensions fuelled a power struggle in the wider region and war broke out. Following a year of fierce battles, the Aztecs surrendered.

1. Festival massacre
In May 1520, Cortés left Tenochtitlan to fight a Spanish force sent to arrest him. In his absence, Aztec nobles celebrating the feast of Toxcatl were massacred by their Spanish guests and Moctezuma was taken captive.

2. Aztec revenge
In response to the massacre, Aztec warriors besieged the Spanish garrison. After Cortés returned, Moctezuma died in unknown circumstances and Cuitlahuac became the new ruler.

3. Spanish flight
In June, the Spanish and allied Tlaxcalans snuck out of the city along the causeway to Tlacopan, laden with gold. Aztec warriors attacked them from canoes, most of the gold fell into the lake, and many people died.

4. Enemy forces
The Aztecs' enemies and oppressed peoples became allies of Spain. Their armies laid siege to Tenochtitlan. Cuitlahuac died of smallpox, a new disease brought by the Spanish, and Cuauhtemoc replaced him as ruler.

5. Attack on Tenochtitlan
In May 1521, the Spanish and their allies attacked Tenochtitlan via the causeway from Iztapalapa, backed by newly built warships. Aztec warriors put up a ferocious defence on the causeway and from canoes.

6. Final battle
After the allied forces took Tenochtitlan's sacred area, the furious battle continued at Tlatelolco. The Aztecs fought on, and Cortés was wounded. But in the end, Aztec warriors, weakened by disease and lack of food after months of siege, were defeated. In August 1521, the last *tlatoani*, Cuauhtemoc, surrendered to the Spanish invaders.

Surviving colonization

The destruction of Tenochtitlan and the brutal Spanish colonization of Mesoamerica ended Aztec rule. But it was not the end of the Nahuas or other peoples. Today, signs of Mexico's Indigenous heritage are everywhere.

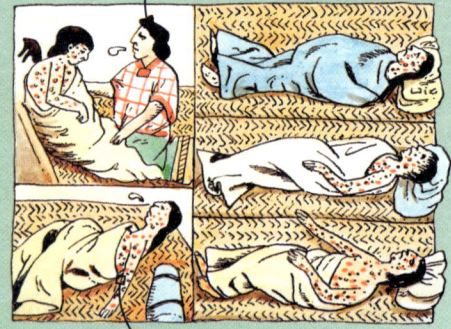

Aztec healer (*ticitl*) has no remedies for imported ills.

Fighting smallpox
The Spanish invaders brought with them new diseases. Indigenous peoples had no immunity to these, and millions died. Aztec healers used their skills and knowledge trying to save their people.

Victim covered in rash typical of smallpox

Spreading Christianity
Catholic priests followed the Spanish invaders from 1524, baptizing Indigenous men, women, and children – some by force, some by choice. Temples were dismantled and the stone used to build churches. Elements of Aztec mythology became mixed with Christian beliefs.

Ehecatl mask burning

Culture lost
Sacred representations of many Aztec deities were destroyed by Catholic missionaries, who wanted to stop the worship of any god but their own.

Monk torching precious artefacts

Holy water, which is added to the wine in a chalice, looks very similar to the goddess Chalchiuhtlicue's swirling river.

Mixed message
Aztec featherwork impressed the Spanish. Soon, local craftspeople were creating objects for Christian rites using feathers. This cover for a chalice features some distinctly Aztec imagery.

Mexican identity

This mural, by the Mexican artist Diego Rivera, celebrates Aztec culture. Painted in 1933, it is part of several scenes depicting Indigenous heritage from across Mexico. It is in Mexico City's Palacio Nacional, which was built in 1529 with stones from Moctezuma II's palace.

Chichi Dog   **Papalotl** Butterfly   **Michin** Fish

Speaking Nahuatl

Several Indigenous languages survive in Mexico, including different forms of Nahuatl, the language of the Aztecs and other Nahua peoples. Today, it is taught in some Mexican schools, and there are lots of online resources, too. Above are three Nahuatl words.

Crown of marigolds and skull face make-up

Fused traditions

The Mexican Day of the Dead is today celebrated in many part of the world. It combines Catholic traditions with echoes of Aztec festivals and the deities linked to them.

Cracking the codex code

Only a handful of Aztec codices exist today. Some were produced by Nahua painter-scribes with Spanish priests, who asked them to write about Aztec life and history for Spanish audiences. Many are known by the names of Europeans who once owned them, or the cities where they are kept.

Codex Boturini
This early codex may predate the invasion. It tells, in pictures, the story of the Aztecs' migration to Tenochtitlan.

These five glyphs depict a five-year stop on the journey.

Codex Mendoza
This codex, created in 1541 for the king of Spain, describes the Aztecs' history and way of life. Nahua scribes painted images and a Spanish priest added text in ink.

Officers are shown with Aztec name glyphs, and descriptions in Spanish.

Florentine Codex

"The General History of the Things of New Spain", commonly known as the "Florentine Codex", is an encyclopedia of Aztec customs, beliefs, flora, fauna, and people, including a history of the Spanish invasion. It was compiled between 1545 and 1577.

The left-hand column translates the Nahuatl into Spanish – not always word for word.

Spanish priests taught Nahua scribes how to write Nahuatl using the Latin alphabet.

1 They gave them the present of gold that they brought... it seemed to them that they were pleased and greatly rejoiced over the gold, for they held it in great esteem.

Translation of Spanish

Two languages
A Spanish priest, Fray Bernardino de Sahagún, worked with a team of Nahua scribes to write text in both Spanish and Nahuatl. The differences in meaning between the two languages are revealing – as in this description of the Aztecs' gift of gold to the invaders.

2 And when they had given the things to them, they seemed to smile, to rejoice and be very happy. Like monkeys they grabbed the gold. ...For gold was what they greatly thirsted for; they were gluttonous for it, starved for it, piggishly wanting it.

Translation of Nahuatl

The right-hand column is written in Nahuatl.

Rediscovering the Aztecs

Most of what we know about the Aztecs comes from codices (singular "codex"). These handwritten books, plus surviving artefacts and archaeological finds, tell us a lot about Aztec history, beliefs, and daily life.

Aztec stone skull racks (see page 99) were among remains unearthed by Mexico City's cathedral.

Buried city

After 1521, the Spanish built Mexico City on the ruins of Tenochtitlan, draining Lake Texcoco. In 1978, road workers in the city centre stumbled upon part of the Great Temple, prompting archaeologists to investigate.

Holes in the head originally held paper decorations or hair.

The god's liver sticks out beneath his skeletal rib cage.

Exciting finds

Archaeologists are gradually revealing more of Tenochtitlan's sacred district, bringing new finds to light. This life-size terracotta statue of the Lord of the Underworld, Mictlantecuhtli, was discovered in 1994.

Travelling treasures

Some of the finest Aztec artworks to survive the Spanish invasion are now in European museum collections. It is thought they were sent to Spain by Hernán Cortés.

This turquoise mosaic mask is in the Pigorini Museum in Rome, Italy.

Glossary

adobe
A mixture of mud and straw dried by the Sun and formed into bricks for construction.

allies
People or city-states working together.

amaranth
A family of plants cultivated for their edible leaves and seeds, which are rich in protein, fibre, and calcium. An Aztec staple food.

ancestor
A distant relative who lived in the past.

anthropology
The study of human beings and their development, social relations, and culture.

appease
To pacify a person or deity.

apprentice
A person who works for a skilled artisan in order to learn and master a trade.

aqueduct
A human-made channel (either raised up or buried underground) that carries water.

archaeologist
A person who excavates ancient sites to reveal their history, by studying the objects and human remains found there.

artefact
An object made by someone, such as a decorative statue, or a useful pot or tool.

artisan
A skilled craftsperson making things by hand.

attribute
A feature of someone or something.

axolotl (ah-SHO-lot)
A salamander native to Mexico and the western USA that, unlike other amphibians, lives its entire life cycle in water.

Aztecs
The name popularly used to refer to the Mexica, a Nahua people who settled in central Mexico in 1325 and built an empire that dominated the region until the Spanish arrived in 1519, defeating them in 1521.

ballgame
A team sport popular among Mesoamerican cultures, including the Aztecs, in which players used the trunk of the body (no hands or feet) to hit a rubber ball and score points.

barter
To exchange goods or services for other goods or services.

basalt
A black rock produced by volcanoes.

batten
In weaving, a long strip of wood used to push the weft yarn, woven through the warp, up against the cloth woven up to that point.

BCE
An abbreviation of the term "Before the Common Era", placed after a date to indicate it happened before the year 0, which is the start of the "Common Era" (CE) in the Western calendar.

blueprint
A plan that is the model for future buildings or town planning.

brazier
A ceramic container for burning coals, used by the Aztecs to burn incense for the gods.

cacao
The raw beans of a tropical tree, used by Mesoamerican peoples to make a drink. Modern cocoa and chocolate are made from cacao beans.

calibrate
To calculate something precisely or measure it against a standard.

causeway
A raised path across water or wet ground.

CE
Abbreviation for "Common Era", used in dates (*see* BCE).

celestial
Relating to the sky, space, or heaven.

censer
A container, sometimes handheld like a ladle, used to burn incense.

ceremonial
Something used for official, religious, or social events.

chalice
A large drinking cup with a stem, used to hold wine during the Christian ceremony of Holy Communion.

chia
A plant of the mint family native to Mexico that is valued for its edible seeds.

city-state
A city, and its surrounding territory, that has its own independent government.

civilization
The culture and way of life of people living together in a complex society.

cochineal
A natural red dye obtained by crushing dried female cochineal insects that feed on cacti.

codex (plural codices)
An ancient, handwritten book. Aztec codices were formed of pages attached in one long strip that folded like a screen, with all the information presented in pictures.

Codex Mendoza
A handwritten book produced in 1541 for King Charles V of Spain that describes the Aztecs' history, way of life, and tribute (tax)

payments. It contains images painted by Nahua scribes and explanatory text in Spanish added by a Spanish priest.

colonization
When one country takes control of another and makes the people who were already there adopt its language and culture.

commoner
In Aztec society, a member of the farming, merchant, or artisan classes.

conquest
In Aztec warfare, the act of defeating a rival city-state to rule over it.

copal
A tree resin burned by the Aztecs to produce a sweet scent as an offering to their gods.

culture
The customs, beliefs, and behaviour shared by a society.

day sign
One of 20 symbols used in combination with 13 numbers to identify each of the 260 days in the Aztec ritual calendar (*tonalpohualli*).

deity
A god or goddess.

diadem
A small crown made of precious materials and worn as an emblem of royalty.

divine
Related to, or provided by, a god or goddess.

ear spool
An ornament inserted into the ear lobe. Also called a plug or gauge.

elite
The most powerful, wealthy, talented, or best-educated people in a society.

embossed
A design, pattern, or lettering that is carved, moulded, or stamped so that it is slightly raised above the surface it decorates.

empire
A group of lands or peoples under the rule of a single government or person (an emperor).

entourage
A group of people, such as attendants or advisers, who accompany an important person when they travel.

era
A long period of time or history, defined by particular features or events.

excrement
Solid waste released by humans and animals via the bowels (poo).

Fifth Sun
The Aztec universe. In Aztec mythology, the gods created and destroyed four worlds (known as "Suns") before creating human life under the Fifth Sun.

flay
To strip the skin off the body of an animal or person. The Aztecs considered the shedding of skins to be a symbol of renewal.

Florentine Codex
A handwritten, illustrated encyclopedia – properly titled "The General History of the Things of New Spain" – of Aztec history, people, beliefs, customs, animals, and plants. It was compiled between 1545 and 1577 by a Spanish priest and Nahua scribes, and contains text in Nahuatl and Spanish.

garrison
A military base or the troops stationed at it.

glyph
A symbol or picture that represents a word, such as those used by Aztec scribes to show the names of specific people and places.

greenstone
A rock with a green colour caused by naturally occurring minerals. The Aztecs associated the colour green with fertility, life, and water.

hygiene
The practice of keeping yourself and your environment clean, to prevent disease.

impersonator
Someone who dresses and acts as someone else. During Aztec rituals, humans who impersonated a deity were believed to take on that god or goddess's identity and powers.

import
To purchase, or bring in via trade, goods and services from other countries.

incense
A substance burned to produce a sweet smell, particularly in sacred places.

Indigenous peoples
The first people to live in a particular place.

jadeite
A hard, green mineral found in part of what is now Guatemala, prized by the Aztecs for its colour, transparency, and rarity.

labret
A piece of jewellery pierced through the lip. Also called a lip plug.

lapidary
A person who specializes in cutting, polishing, and setting gemstones.

loincloth
A piece of cloth passed through the legs and tied around the hips, sometimes worn by men in hot countries as their only item of clothing.

loom
A frame used to weave thread into cloth. Aztec weavers used a backstrap loom, attached around their waist at one end and to a post at the other.

maguey (ma-GAY)
The Spanish name for a native American plant from the agave family with coarse fibres and thorny leaves. It was cultivated by the Aztecs to produce textiles, rope, and alcohol, among other things.

massacre
The killing, usually brutally, of a large number of people at the same time.

merchant
A person who buys, sells, or exchanges goods, sometimes travelling to trade.

Mesoamerica
A historical and cultural region stretching from modern-day central Mexico to northern Costa Rica, where several civilizations (including the Olmecs, Maya, and Aztecs) emerged in the centuries before the Spanish invasion.

Mexica (Meh-SHEE-kah)
The name by which the Aztec people called themselves, referring to their ethnic group.

migration
The movement of people from one dwelling place to live in another region or country.

missionary
Someone sent to another country to convert the people living there to their religion.

Mixtec
An Indigenous people who in Aztec times had a reputation for skilful goldworking.

mohican
A hairstyle in which the sides of the head are shaved, leaving a narrow strip of hair along the centre of the head that is usually styled to stand upright.

mythology
The ancient stories (myths) told by a people to explain their origins and the world around them, often involving that people's gods, goddesses, and legendary heroes.

Nahua (NAH-wa)
Indigenous Nahuatl-speaking peoples from Mesoamerica, among them the Aztecs.

Nahuatl (NAH-wat)
The language spoken by Nahua peoples, including the Aztecs.

noble
A member of the nobility, with more rights and privileges than commoners.

novice
Someone who is new to, or has little experience in, a job, skill, or situation.

obsidian
A glass-like volcanic rock.

offering
Something given to gods in worship.

Order of Eagles and Jaguars
A group of skilful Aztec warriors who, in reward for excellent military performance, earned the noble rank of *cuauhocelotl* (a Nahuatl word meaning "eagle-jaguar").

pectoral
A piece of jewellery worn over the chest, attached to a necklace.

pictogram
A picture or symbol that represents a word, thing, or idea.

pigment
A substance that gives other materials a particular colour.

pulque (POOL-kay)
The Spanish name for an alcoholic drink made from the fermented sap of the maguey plant.

quetzal
A tropical bird from Central and South America with vividly coloured, shimmering feathers greatly prized by the Aztecs.

regalia
The clothes and objects a person wears or carries as emblems of their role as ruler.

replica
An exact copy of something.

resin
A sticky substance produced by some trees – for example, pine or copal resin.

ritual
A set of words and/or actions that are always performed the same way – for example, in a religious ceremony.

ritual sacrifice
A ceremonial act in which offerings of food, flowers, paper, incense, animals, or humans are made as a gift to a deity.

sacred
Holy or with religious significance, possibly related to a god or goddess.

scribe
A person whose job it was to write and copy documents by hand. Before the Spanish invasion, Aztec scribes conveyed information through painted pictures, not written words.

siege
The surrounding and blockading of a town or fortified structure in order to conquer it.

society
A group of people who live together or who are involved together in a community.

soothsayer
A person believed to have the power to see into the future and predict what will happen.

spindle
A rod used to twist raw maguey fibre, cotton, or wool into thread when spinning by hand.

submission
The act of allowing someone or something to defeat or control you.

tamale (ta-MAH-lay)
A parcel of maize flour dough stuffed with a filling, then wrapped in maize husks or banana leaves and steamed. Popular among the Aztecs, and still eaten in modern Mexico.

temple
A building for religious ceremonies.

tortilla (tor-TEE-yah)
A thin, round flatbread traditionally made from maize flour and cooked on a griddle.

trecena (treh-SAY-na)
A Spanish word referring to one of 20 periods of 13 days in the Aztec ritual calendar (*tonalpohualli*).

tribute
In the Aztec empire, a tax paid to the Aztec rulers by the city-states they controlled.

Triple Alliance
The name of the alliance formed in 1428 between the rulers of the city-states of Tenochtitlan, Texcoco, and Tlacopan, who united to defeat the Tepanecs.

veintena (bayn-TEH-na)
A Spanish word referring to one of 18 periods of 20 days in the Aztec solar calendar (*xiuhpohualli*).

vigil
The act of staying awake and alert to pray or prepare for a religious festival.

wattle and daub
A type of wall consisting of interwoven twigs plastered with a mixture of clay and straw.

Speak like an Aztec

The Aztec language, called Nahuatl, can be written in our alphabet, but some letters are pronounced differently. The following guide will help English speakers to say Nahuatl words – more or less – like an Aztec.

Nahuatl letter(s)	Sounds like:
c	"s" before "e" or "i", or "k"
cu / uc	"kw" in "queen"
hu / uh	"w" in water
i	"ee" in feet
ll	long "l" in "silly"
qu	"k" before "e" or "i", or "kw" in "queen"
tl	"t" in "cat"
tz	"ts" in "sits"
x	"sh" in "shine"
z	"s" in "Sun"

Below is a glossary of some of the Nahuatl words that appear in this book, with their pronunciation in brackets. When speaking Nahuatl, the emphasis usually falls on the second-to-last syllable of the word.

altepetl (al-TEH-pet)
Literally, a "water hill". A community with its own government, similar to a city-state.

amantecatl (ah-man-TEH-cat)
Artisans who specialized in featherwork.

cacahuatl (kah-KAH-wat)
Raw cacao beans and the drink made by crushing them with water and spices.

calli (KAL-lee)
A house.

calmecac (kal-MEH-kak)
A school for noble boys, run by priests, where they learned writing, astronomy, and law, and could train to become priests.

chimalli (chee-MAH-lee)
A shield used in warfare, representing war.

chinampa (chee-NAM-pa)
An artificial island created in shallow water and filled with soil to grow crops.

cihuacoatl (see-wah-KO-at)
The most important official in the Aztec empire after the ruler (*tlatoani*), named after Earth goddess Cihuacoatl ("Woman Snake").

coatl (KO-at)
Serpent or snake.

cueitl (KWAY-eet)
A skirt.

cuicacalli (kwee-ka-KAL-lee)
The "House of Song", where young people learned to sing, dance, and play instruments.

cuicatlamatiliztli (kwee-kat-la-mat-eel-EES-tlee)
Literally, the "art of song", meaning music.

huehuetl (WEH-weht)
An upright drum played with the hands.

huipilli (wee-PEE-lee)
A tunic-shaped blouse. The main garment worn by Aztec women, over a skirt (*cueitl*).

itztli (EETS-tlee)
Obsidian, or a knife made of obsidian.

macehualtin (mah-seh-WAHL-teen)
People of the Aztec "commoner" class.

macuahuitl (mak-WAH-weet)
A club-like weapon with sharp obsidian blades wielded in hand-to-hand combat.

maquizcoatl (mak-weez-KO-at)
A two-headed serpent. Also slang for gossip.

maxtlatl (MASHT-lat)
A loincloth, worn by Aztec men on its own or with a cloak (*tilmatli*).

nahualli (nah-WAL-lee)
A man or woman with the power to transform themself into an animal.

ollamaliztli (oh-lah-mah-LEES-tlee)
The Aztec version of the ballgame.

pipiltin (pee-PEEL-teen)
People of the Aztec noble class.

pochteca (poch-TEH-ka)
Merchants who travelled long distances to trade goods on behalf of the Aztec empire.

tecpatl (TEK-pat)
Flint, or a knife made of flint.

telpochcalli (tel-poch-KAL-lee)
A school for boys of the commoner class, where they trained to become warriors.

teotl (TAY-oht)
Deities and their sacred energy, believed by the Aztecs to exist all around them. People and nature were aspects of this divine force.

teponaztli (te-poh-NATS-tlee)
A horizontal drum played with sticks.

ticitl (TEE-seet)
A community healer, who used herbal knowledge, practical experience, and magic to treat illnesses and injuries.

tilmatli (teel-MAHT-lee)
A cloak worn by Aztec boys and men.

tlahuiztli (tlah-WEETS-lee)
A body suit, often covered with colourful feathers, worn by certain warriors, generally over quilted cotton armour (*ichcahuipilli*). Also a warrior's insignia and other gear.

tlatoani (tlah-toh-AH-nee)
Literally, "he who speaks". The ruler of a city-state (*altepetl*).

tlaxilacalli (tla-shee-la-KAL-lee)
A neighbourhood in a city-state (*altepetl*) managed by a noble lord who provided the commoners with work in return for tribute.

tonalco (toh-NAL-koh)
The annual dry season.

tonalli (toh-NAL-lee)
Spiritual energy or life force, understood by the Aztecs to be present in all things.

tonalpohualli (toh-nal-poh-WAL-lee)
The Aztec 260-day ritual calendar, made up of 20 periods of 13 days.

topilli (toh-PEEL-lee)
A staff carried as an emblem of authority.

tzitzimime (tsee-tsee-MEE-meh)
A female being that the Aztecs believed would descend from the sky to eat human beings during solar eclipses and other times when the future of the world was uncertain.

xiuhcoatl (shoo-KO-at)
A fire serpent.

xiuhamolli (shoo-wah-MOL-lee)
A flowering plant (soapwort in English), which contains grease-dissolving chemicals.

xiuhpohualli (shoo-po-WAH-lee)
The Aztec solar calendar of 365 days, composed of 18 periods of 20 days called *veintenas*, plus five days at the year's end.

xopan (SHO-pan)
The annual wet season.

Index

Page numbers in **bold** are for main topics.

A
Acamapichtli (ruler) 66
Ahuitzotl (ruler) 66, 67
alcohol 76, 118
algae cakes 106, 119
amaranth seeds 115
animal skins 78
apprenticeships 74–75, 107
archers 86
armour, cotton 78, 86
artisans 62, **90–91**, 131
astronomy 24, 75, 89
Aubin Tonalamatl 138–139
avocados 115
Axayacatl (ruler) 66, 67
Aztec empire **8–11**, 12–13, 16, **28–29**
   end of 146–149
Aztlan 9, 12

B
ballgame 19, 25, 97, **142–143**
bathing 122
beans 107, 114, 115
birds 108, 130–131
birthdays 47
books **136–137**, 138–139, 152
botanical gardens 96, 120
boys 73, **74–75**, 124, 128

C
cacao beans 25, 108, 115, 119
calendar stone **36–37**
calendars
   ritual calendar **46–47**, 54, 88, 139
   solar calendar 47, **50–51**, 54
canals 94, **104–105**, 112–113
canoes 75, 105, 113
captives 69, 80, 82–83, 129
causeways 8, 94, 105
Chalchiuhtlicue (goddess) 42
chia seeds 115
Chicomecoatl (goddess) 50–51, 53, 116–117, 138–139
childbirth 72, 123

children 19, 54, **72–77**
chillies 114, 116, 119
Chimalpopoca (ruler) 66, 137
chinampas 95, **112–113**
chocolate (cacao beans) 25, 108, 115, 119
Christianity 150
Cihuacoatl (goddess) 51, 52, 68, 116
cihuacoatl (deputy ruler) 68
Cinteotl (god) 50, 116, 117
cities 28–29
   Teotihuacan **20–21**, 22–23, Tlatelolco 94, 106–107
   see also Tenochtitlan (city)
classes **62–63**
   merchants and artisans **90–91**
   nobles and commoners **68–69**, 70–71, 74–75, 124, 126
   priests **88–89**
   rulers **64–67**
   warriors **80–87**
Coatlicue (goddess) 40, 43, 45, 99
codex (codices) 11, 136–137, **152–153**
Codex Mendoza 11, 137, 152
colonization **150–151**
Columbus, Christopher 146
commoners 62–63, **68–69**, 74–75, 80, 95
   dress 124, 126, 128
conches 86, 108, 126, 132
coronation ceremonies 65, **100–101**
Cortés, Hernán 146–149
cotton 78, 115, 124–125, 127
Coyolxauhqui (goddess) 43, 99
creation stories **32–35**, 37
crops 112, **114–115**, 116–117
Cuauhtemoc (ruler) 66, 149
Cuitlahuac (ruler) 66, 148–149

D
days, calendar 46–47, 50, 139
death rituals 11, 52, 56–57, 151

diet 112, **114–115**, **118–119**
domestic life 38, 73, 77
   homes 68, 69, 95, **104–105**
dress 81, **124–127**, 130–131
   hair 83, 88, 122, **128–129**
   headdresses 101, 130–131
drink 25, 76, 118, 119
drums 86, 89, 140

E
eagles 11, 47, 81, 87
eagle warriors 81, 83, 87
ear piercing 76
education 73, **74–75**
Ehecatl (god) 33, 35, 42, 82, 121, 126, 132, 133
enslavement 69, 147
   see also captives

F
fans 131
farming 62, **112–113**, 114–117
feathers 78, 81, 82–87, 108, **130–131**
featherworkers 74, 91, 131, 150
festivals **52–55**, 70–71, 76, 116–117, 148
   see also calendars
Fifth Sun **34–35**, 36
fire 38, 54–55
fishing 104, 105
Florentine Codex 65, 69, 81, 118, 123, 129, 131, 152
flowers 114, 119, 120–121, 122
flowery wars 86
flutes 140
food 107, 112, **114–115**, **118–119**

G
gender roles 72
generals (warriors) 84–85, 86
girls 73, **76–77**, 124, 129
glyphs 24, 136
gods and goddesses 10, 38–39, **42–45**
   calendars 46–47, 50–51
   creation stories 32–37
   festivals 52–53, 116–117
   fire gods 48–49
   gold 134
   healing 121, 123
   masks 58–59
   music 141

New Fire ceremony 54–55
   sacrifice 56–57
   serpents 40–41
   see also priests; temples
gold 91, 109, **134–135**, 152
goldsmiths 75, 91, 108
"great speakers" **64–65**
greenstone 126, 132

H
hair 83, 88, 122, **128–129**
harvest 53, 116–117
headdresses 101, 130–131
healers 89, 121
health and hygiene **120–123**
herbal remedies **120–121**
homes 38, 68, 69, 95, **104–105**
Huehueteotl (god) 38, 49, 50
Huitzilopochtli (god) 11, 27, **33**, 38, 40–41, 51, 53, 98–99, 101
human sacrifice **56–57**, 69, 99

I
illness 120–121
impersonators 58, 89
   see also masks
incense 88, 106, 132
Itzcoatl (ruler) 29, 66
Ixtlilton (god) 121

J
jadeite 132, 134
jaguars 19, 39, 47, 81, 83
jaguar warriors 81, 83
jewellery 40–41, 126, 132–133, 135

K
knives 56–57, 132–133

L
language 9, 136–137, 151, 152
lapidaries 75, 90
law and order 62
lip plugs 64, 109, 126, 133, 134–135

M
maguey plant 39, 78, 107, 115, 120, 124–125
maize 39, 52, 106, 115, **116–117** 118
Malintzin (Malinche) 147
maps 8–9, 12–13, 16–17, 63, 102–103
markets 96, **106–107**, 108
marriage 67, 77, 129

masks 21, **58–59**, 81, 133
masons 91
Maya civilization 17, 21, **24–25**, 147
meat 119
medicine 114, **120–121**
merchants 62–63, **90–91**, 97, 107, 108, 125
Mesoamerican civilizations 9, **16–17**
   Maya 17, 21, **24–25**, 147
   Mixtec 10, 16, 108, 136
   Olmec 16, **18–19**, 21, 142
   Teotihuacan 16, **20–21**, 22–23, 25
   Zapotec 16
   see also Aztec empire; Nahua peoples
Mexica peoples 9
Mexico 8–9, 12, 98, 151, 153
Mictlancihuatl (goddess) 43
Mictlantecuhtli (god) 43, 57, 58, 153
migrations 9, 12–13, 27, 152
mirrors 33, 132
Mixcoatl (god) 40, 45
Mixtec civilization 16, 108
Moctezuma I, Ilhuicamina 64, 66, 120
Moctezuma II 66, 96, 105, 147–148
   coronation 65, **100–101**
"Moctezuma's headdress" 130–131
Moon, the 35
murals 20, 151
music 74, **140–141**
mythical beasts
   serpents 21, **40–41**, 98, 134
   were-jaguars 19, 39

N
Nahua peoples 9, 12, **26–27**, **150–151**
Nahuatl (language) 9, 136–137, 151, 152
naming ceremonies 72
Nanahuatzin (god) 34–35, 133
neck stretching 76
New Fire ceremony 11, **54–55**
Nezahualcoyotl (ruler) 28
nobles 62–63, 67, **68–69**, 70–71, 80, 82–83
   dress 125, 126–127
   women and children 74–75, 78–79, 125

O
obsidian 56, 86–87, 132
Olmec civilization 16, **18–19**, 21, 142

P
palaces 96
popcorn 118
priests **88–89**
   ceremonies 53, 54–55, 57
   dress 58–59, 128, 150
   see also temples
pyramids 21, 22–23, 98–99

Q
Quetzalcoatl (god) 33, 40, 97, 116, 121, 126, 132, 133

R
ritual calendar **46–47**, 54, 88, 139
ritual sacrifice 11, **56–57**, 69, 99, 101
rubber production 19, 143
rulers 10, 29, 62–63, **64–67**, 68
   see also Moctezuma II

S
sacrifice 11, **56–57**, 69, 99, 101
schooling 74–75, 125
scribes 74, 136, 152
seasons 51, 53, 116–117
serpents (snakes) 21, **40–41**, 98, 134
shape-shifting gods 39
shells 86, 108, 126, 133
Shield Jaguar II 24
shields 80, 82–83, 84–85, 87, 131
skulls 58–59, 99, 153
slavery see enslavement
smallpox 149, 150
snakes (serpents) 21, **40–41**, 98, 134
society **62–63**
   children **72–77**
   merchants and artisans **90–91**
   nobles and commoners **68–69**, 70–71, 74–75
   priests **88–89**
   rulers **64–67**
   war and warriors **80–87**
women 38, **76–79**, 89
solar calendar 47, **50–51**, 54
songs 140–141
soothsayers 47, 89, 132
Spanish 10, 102, **146–149**, 152
spies 86, 91
spinning 72, 73, 78–79
sports 25, 97, **142–143**
squashes 107, 114, 115
steam rooms 122–123
stonecutters 75, 90
storytelling 12–13, 136
Sun, the 35, 54
Suns (Aztec worlds) 32, **34–35**, 36
Sun stone **36–37**
supernatural beings 39, 123
sweeping 53, 75, 95, 122

T
tamales 77, 106, 118
teachers 62, 125
Tecuhciztecatl (god) 34–35
temples 22–23, **96–99**, 100–101
Tenochtitlan (city) 8, 28–29, **94–95**, 104–105
   founding of 11, 12–13
   map 102–103
   market 106–107
   rediscovery of 153
   rulers 65, 66–67, 71
   Spanish invasion 147, 148–149, 150
   temples 96–99, 100–101
   Great Temple **98–99**
trade 108–109
Teotihuacan 16, **20–21**, 22–23, 25
Tepanec people 27, 28–29
Texcoco, Lake 8, 28–29, 105, 112
textiles 78–79, 106, 115, 124–125, 127
Tezcatlipoca (god) **32–33**, 51, 59
Tikal (city) 25
Tizoc (ruler) 66, 67
Tlacopan (city) 28
Tlaloc (god) 10, 42, 53, 50–51, 56, 98–99, 116–117, 139
Tlaltecuhtli (goddess) 44
Tlatelolco (city) 66, 67, 94, 106–107
Tlaxcala people 146–148
Tlazolteotl (goddess) 44, 123
tomatoes 114
Tonatiuh (god) 35, 36, 97
tortillas 118
trade **108–109**, 119
   markets 106–107
   see also merchants
treasures 58, 119, **130–135**, 153
trecenas (calendar periods) 47
tribute 10, **108–109**
Triple Alliance 28
turquoise regalia 63, 64, 100
turquoise stone 10, 40–41, 59, 108, 132–133, 153

V
vanilla 115, 119
veintenas (calendar periods) 50–51, 52, 116–117
vendors 106–107

W
warfare 80, **86–87**, 148–149
warriors 62–63, 75, **80–85**, 87, 89, 128
washing 122
water boatmen 119
weapons 80–81, 82, 85, **86–87**
weaving 63, 73, **78–79**
wedding ceremonies 77
   see also marriage
were-jaguars 19, 39
women 38, **76–79**, 89
   dress 124–127, 129
   pregnancy and childbirth 54, 72, 123
writing 24, **136–137**, 138–139

X
Xilonen (goddess) 51, 117
Xipe Totec (god) 33, 50, 57, 89
Xiuhtecuhtli (god) 41, 44, 49, 51
Xochipilli (god) 45, 132, 141

Y
Yacatecuhtli (god) 45, 90, 97
years, calendar 11, 51, 137

Z
Zapotec civilization 16
zoo 96

Acknowledgements

Dorling Kindersley would like to thank:
Christine Stroyan for proofreading; Elizabeth Wise for indexing; Steve Crozier for creative retouching; Gabriel Midgley for visualizations; Simon Mumford for maps; and Priya Singh for additional picture research and Samrajkumar S for picture credits.

The publisher would like to thank the following for their kind permission to reproduce their photographs:
(Key: a-above; b-below/bottom; c-centre; f-far; l-left; r-right; t-top)

1-160 Dreamstime.com: Yuls2000 (Background). **1 Alamy Stock Photo:** Geogphotos. **3 The Metropolitan Museum of Art:** Purchase, 2015 Benefit Fund and Lila Acheson Wallace Gift, 2016 (b). **6 Bridgeman Images:** © NPL - DeA Picture Library / © A. De Gregorio. **8 Alamy Stock Photo:** Christina Felschen (br). **9 Bridgeman Images:** (bl). **© The Trustees of the British Museum. All rights reserved. Library of Congress, Washington, D.C.:** Codex Azcatitlan (br). **10 Bridgeman Images:** © NPL - DeA Picture Library / © A. De Gregorio (bl). **Library of Congress, Washington, D.C.:** Codex Azcatitlan (cla); Codex Azcatitlan (br). **Shutterstock.com:** Gianni Dagli Orti (cra). **11 Alamy Stock Photo:** Realy Easy Star. **12-13 Alamy Stock Photo:** ART Collection. **15 Getty Images:** Universal Images Group / Werner Forman. **16 Alamy Stock Photo:** EDU Vision (cra); Kumar Sriskandan (bl); Smith Archive (br). **Getty Images:** De Agostini Picture Library (tc). **17 Getty Images:** Universal Images Group / Werner Forman (c). **18 Getty Images:** Universal Images Group / Werner Forman (c). **19 Alamy Stock Photo:** Stefano Ravera (cl). **The Metropolitan Museum of Art:** The Michael C. Rockefeller Memorial Collection, Bequest of Nelson A. Rockefeller, 1979 (br). **20 Alamy Stock Photo:** Ivan Vdovin (c). **20-21 Alamy Stock Photo:** Michael Rooney (b). **21 Bridgeman Images:** © Iberfoto (tl). **Getty Images:** Moment Open / Oliver J Davis Photography (cra). **22-23 Getty Images:** Moment / Max Shen. **24 Alamy Stock Photo:** Chronicle (br). **Getty Images:** De Agostini / Dea / G. Dagli Orti (c). **25 Adobe Stock:** SL-Photography (tl). **Getty Images / iStock:** E+ / DSMPics (tr). **Getty Images:** Universal Images Group / Werner Forman (br). **26 Alamy Stock Photo:** The Picture Art Collection (b). **27 Alamy Stock Photo:** Album (bl); Panther Media Global / Jgaunion (cla); GRANGER - Historical Picture Archive (ca); GRANGER - Historical Picture Archive (cra). **Getty Images:** De Agostini / Dea / G. Dagli Orti (br). **28 Alamy Stock Photo:** ART Collection (cla); History_Docu_Photo (br). **29 Alamy Stock Photo:** Circle Archive (tc); Science History Images (b). **30-31 Library of Congress, Washington, D.C.:** Carol M Highsmith. **35 Alamy Stock Photo:** The History Collection (tc). **Getty Images:** Universal Images Group / Werner Forman (tl). **36-37 Library of Congress, Washington, D.C.:** Carol M Highsmith (c). **37 Alamy Stock Photo:** The Picture Art Collection (c). **Getty Images:** Hulton Archive / Ewing Galloway (br). **38 Alamy Stock Photo:** ART Collection (cl). **Getty Images:** De Agostini / Dea / G. Dagli Orti (cr). **Library of Congress, Washington, D.C.:** Bernardino De Sahagún (tl). **39 Alamy Stock Photo:** Historic Images (bc); Logic Images (cra). **Dreamstime.com:** Andrii Zhezhera (bl). **Getty Images:** Universal Images Group / Werner Forman (tl). **40-41 Dreamstime.com:** Mistervlad. **41 Alamy Stock Photo:** Historic Collection (tc); Peter Horree (tl). **46 Alamy Stock Photo:** History and Art Collection (cla, br/x3); The History Collection (ca/x4); The History Collection (c/x4); History and Art Collection (cr, clb/x3); The History Collection (crb/x2, bl/x2). **47 Alamy Stock Photo:** History and Art Collection (cra/1); The History Collection (cra/2); History and Art Collection (cra/3); The History Collection (cra/4). **Library of Congress, Washington, D.C.:** Bernardino De Sahagún (c, bl, bc/br). **48-49 Bridgeman Images:** GEO Image Collection / Kenneth Garrett. **50 Alamy Stock Photo:** Science History Images (bl). **Biodiversity Heritage Library:** Smithsonian Libraries and Archives (ca); Smithsonian Libraries and Archives (cra); Smithsonian Libraries and Archives (fcra); Smithsonian Libraries and Archives (fcl); Smithsonian Libraries and Archives (cl); Smithsonian Libraries and Archives (c); Smithsonian Libraries and Archives (cr); Smithsonian Libraries and Archives (fcr). **51 Biodiversity Heritage Library:** Smithsonian Libraries and Archives (cla); Smithsonian Libraries and Archives (fcla); Smithsonian Libraries and Archives (ca); Smithsonian Libraries and Archives (cra); Smithsonian Libraries and Archives (fcra); Smithsonian Libraries and Archives (fcl); Smithsonian Libraries and Archives (cl); Smithsonian Libraries and Archives (c); Smithsonian Libraries and Archives (cr); Smithsonian Libraries and Archives (fcr). **© The Trustees of the British Museum. All rights reserved:** (cb). **52 Alamy Stock Photo:** Historic Collection. **53 Alamy Stock Photo:** Art Collection 2 (tr, c); Art Collection 2 (bc); Science History Images (br). **56 Alamy Stock Photo:** Art Collection 2 (cla); J.Enrique Molina (bc). **Getty Images:** De Agostini / Dea / G. Dagli Orti (cr). **Library of Congress, Washington, D.C.:** Bernardino De Sahagún (bl). **56-57 Getty Images:** Universal Images Group / Werner Forman (bc). **57 Alamy Stock Photo:** Album (br); Historic Collection (t). **58-59 © The Trustees of the British Museum. All rights reserved. 58 Alamy Stock Photo:** Peter Horree (bc). **Getty Images:** De Agostini / Dea / A. De Gregorio (cl); De Agostini / Dea / G. Dagli Orti (cr). **60-61 Library of Congress, Washington, D.C.:** Bernardino De Sahagún. **62 Library of Congress, Washington, D.C.:** (cla). **63 Library of Congress, Washington, D.C.:** (tr). **64 Alamy Stock Photo:** Steeve-X-Art. **65 Alamy Stock Photo:** Realy Easy Star (c). **Library of Congress, Washington, D.C.:** Bernardino De Sahagún (clb, bl); Bernardino De Sahagún (crb). **66 Alamy Stock Photo:** The Picture Art Collection (c); The History Collection (bc). **Library of Congress, Washington, D.C.:** Bernardino De Sahagún. **67 Alamy Stock Photo:** GRANGER - Historical Picture Archive (bc); Zoom Historical (cra); Vibrant Pictures (cr). **© The Trustees of the British Museum. All rights reserved. Library of Congress, Washington, D.C.:** Codex Azcatitlan (cla). **68 Alamy Stock Photo:** Album (br). **Library of Congress, Washington, D.C.:** Bernardino De Sahagún (cla); Bernardino De Sahagún (bl); Bernardino De Sahagún (cra). **The Metropolitan Museum of Art:** The Michael C. Rockefeller Memorial Collection, Bequest of Nelson A. Rockefeller, 1979 (bc). **69 Alamy Stock Photo:** Mostardi Photography (c). **Library of Congress, Washington, D.C.:** Bernardino De Sahagún (cra); Bernardino De Sahagún (br). **The Metropolitan Museum of Art:** Bequest of Arthur M. Bullowa, 1993 (cr); Museum Purchase, 1900 (cl). **70-71 Alamy Stock Photo:** The Picture Art Collection. **72 Alamy Stock Photo:** The Picture Art Collection (c). **The Cleveland Museum Of Art:** Gift of Edward B. Greene (cr). **73 Alamy Stock Photo:** CalimaX (cl); History & Art Collection (t); Photo12 / Ann Ronan Picture Library (cr, b). **74 Alamy Stock Photo:** History & Art Collection (c). **74-75 Bridgeman Images:** © Bodleian Libraries, University of Oxford (b). **75 Alamy Stock Photo:** History & Art Collection (ca). **Bridgeman Images:** © Bodleian Libraries, University of Oxford (c/clb); © Bodleian Libraries, University of Oxford (crb). **76 Alamy Stock Photo:** The History Collection (t). **Library of Congress, Washington, D.C.:** Bernardino De Sahagún (b/x3). **77 Alamy Stock Photo:** The Picture Art Collection. **78 Alamy Stock Photo:** Heritage Image Partnership Ltd / index (clb). **Benson Latin American Collection, LLILAS Benson Latin American Studies and Collections, The. University of Texas at Austin:** (br). **Bridgeman Images:** © Bodleian Libraries, University of Oxford (c/Cotton). **Getty Images:** De Agostini / Dea / G. Dagli Orti (c); Universal Images Group / Photo 12 (cla, cra). **79 Benson Latin American Collection, LLILAS Benson Latin American Studies and Collections, The. University of Texas at Austin:** (b). **Bridgeman Images:** © Bodleian Libraries, University of Oxford (tr). **Library of Congress, Washington, D.C.:** Bernardino De Sahagún (tl); Bernardino De Sahagún (c). **80 Alamy Stock Photo:** Realy Easy Star (c). **Library of Congress, Washington, D.C.:** Bernardino De Sahagún (bl); Bernardino De Sahagún (bc). **81 Alamy Stock Photo:** Geogphotos. **82-83 Bridgeman Images:** © Bodleian Libraries, University of Oxford (b). **83 Alamy Stock Photo:** ART Collection (ca); Kumar Sriskandan (cra). **84-85 Bridgeman Images:** © Bodleian Libraries, University of Oxford. **86 Alamy Stock Photo:** EDU Vision (crb); Wiliam Perry (br). **Bridgeman Images:** © Museum of Fine Arts, Boston (bl). **Library of Congress, Washington, D.C.:** Bernardino De Sahagún (cl, tl). **87 Alamy Stock Photo:** Smith Archive (tc). **Getty Images:** De Agostini / Dea / G. Dagli Orti (cb). **88 Alamy Stock Photo:** Heritage Image Partnership Ltd / Index (br). **Bridgeman Images:** © NPL - DeA Picture Library / G. Dagli Orti (bl). **Dreamstime.com:** Whpics (cr). **Library of Congress, Washington, D.C.:** Bernardino De Sahagún (cla). **89 Alamy Stock Photo:** Heritage Image Partnership Ltd / Index (tl); Prisma Archivo (r); Icom Images (clb). **Bridgeman Images:** © Bodleian Libraries, University of Oxford (c). **Library of Congress, Washington, D.C.:** Bernardino De Sahagún (bc). **90 Library of Congress, Washington, D.C.:** Bernardino De Sahagún (cl, cra); Bernardino De Sahagún (b). **91 Library of Congress, Washington, D.C.:** Bernardino De Sahagún (tl, tr, b); Bernardino De Sahagún (br); Bernardino De Sahagún (cla, cra). **94-95 Alamy Stock Photo:** CalimaX. **95 Alamy Stock Photo:** Ann Ronan Picture Library / Heritage-ImagesThe Print Collector (tc). **Library of Congress, Washington, D.C.:** Bernardino De Sahagún (tl). **96 Bridgeman Images:** © Bodleian Libraries, University of Oxford (bl). **Library of Congress, Washington, D.C.:** Bernardino De Sahagún (br). **98 Alamy Stock Photo:** Jeffrey Isaac Greenberg 11+ (cla). **Dreamstime.com:** William Perry (tr). **Getty Images:** De Agostini / Dea / G. Dagli Orti (tc). **Getty Images / iStock:** Nathan Kelly (ca). **99 Getty Images:** De Agostini / Dea / G. Dagli Orti (bc); Universal Images Group / Werner Forman (cra). **100 Alamy Stock Photo:** Granger - Historical Picture Archive (cl). **101 Alamy Stock Photo:** Album (cr). **102-103 Alamy Stock Photo:** Science History Images / Photo Researchers. **105 Alamy Stock Photo:** Heritage Image Partnership Ltd / Index (tr); World History Archive (cr). **Getty Images:** De Agostini / Dea / G. Dagli Orti (br). **108 Alamy Stock Photo:** Kit Day (r); Jon G. Fuller / VWPics (bl). **Dorling Kindersley:** University of Aberdeen / Gary Ombler (clb). **Library of Congress, Washington, D.C.:** Bernardino De Sahagún (cla). **MAS. IB.2010.017.064, Collection Paul & Dora Janssen-Art, Flemish Community, Brussels, Photo: Hugo Maertens:** (cb). **109 Alamy Stock Photo:** History & Art Collection. **110-111 Alamy Stock Photo:** YA / BOT. **115 Bridgeman Images:** © Bodleian Libraries, University of Oxford (ca). **Library of Congress, Washington, D.C.:** Bernardino De Sahagún (cla). **116 Alamy Stock Photo:** World History Archive (bl); YA / BOT (tr). **Library of Congress, Washington, D.C.:** Bernardino De Sahagún. **117 Alamy Stock Photo:** Art Collection 2 (cra); Peter Horree (bl); The History Collection (br). **Bridgeman Images:** © Boltin Picture Library (tl). **The Metropolitan Museum of Art:** Museum Purchase, 1900 (tc). **118 Alamy Stock Photo:** The Picture Art Collection (bl). **Library of Congress, Washington, D.C.:** Bernardino De Sahagún (c). **119 Bridgeman Images:** © Brooklyn Museum / Museum Collection Fund (bl). **Dreamstime.com:** Whpics (br). **Library of Congress, Washington, D.C.:** Bernardino De Sahagún (tc). **Shutterstock.com:** EQRoy (c). **120 Library of Congress, Washington, D.C.:** Bernardino De Sahagún (x4); Bernardino De Sahagún (tc/cra). **121 Alamy Stock Photo:** History and Art Collection (cl); Panther Media Global / Jgaunion (cr). **122 Alamy Stock Photo:** Historic Collection (b). **Library of Congress, Washington, D.C.:** Bernardino De Sahagún (cla); Bernardino De Sahagún (ca). **123 Adobe Stock:** Gerardo Borbolla (l). **Alamy Stock Photo:** ART Collection (br). **Library of Congress, Washington, D.C.:** Bernardino De Sahagún (t/x3). **126 Alamy Stock Photo:** Penta Springs Limited / Artokoloro (tl). **Art Institvte Chicago:** Gift of Mrs. L. A. Coonley Ward (tr). **© The Trustees of the British Museum. All rights reserved. Getty Images:** Universal Images Group / Werner Forman (tc); Universal Images Group / Werner Forman (crb). **The Metropolitan Museum of Art:** Gift of the Mol Collection, 2020 (clb); The Michael C. Rockefeller Memorial Collection, Purchase, Nelson A. Rockefeller Gift, 1967 (cla). **127 Brooklyn Museum:** Gift in memory of Elizabeth Ege Freudenheim (c). **Library of Congress, Washington, D.C.:** Bernardino De Sahagún (b/x4). **129 Bridgeman Images:** © Bodleian Libraries, University of Oxford (tc). **130 Alamy Stock Photo:** Science History Images / Photo Researchers (tl). **130-131 Alamy Stock Photo:** Associated Press / Ronald Zak (b). **131 Alamy Stock Photo:** GRANGER - Historical Picture Archive (tl); Mostardi Photography (bc). **Library of Congress, Washington, D.C.:** Bernardino De Sahagún (r). **132 Alamy Stock Photo:** Carver Mostardi (c); Carver Mostardi (bc). **© The Trustees of the British Museum. All rights reserved. The Cleveland Museum Of Art:** Gift of James C. Gruener in memory of his wife, Florence Crowell Gruener (cra). **Getty Images:** De Agostini / Dea Picture Library (cla). **The Metropolitan Museum of Art:** Gift of John and Marisol Stokes, 2012 (br). **133 Alamy Stock Photo:** World History Archive (br). **© The Trustees of the British Museum. All rights reserved. Getty Images:** Universal Images Group / Werner Forman (cb). **Princeton University Art Museum:** Museum purchase, gift of Herbert L. Lucas, Class of 1950 (tr). **Shutterstock.com:** Gianni Dagli Orti (bc). **134 Alamy Stock Photo:** John Mitchell (cl). **Library of Congress, Washington, D.C.. The Metropolitan Museum of Art:** Purchase, 2015 Benefit Fund and Lila Acheson Wallace Gift, 2016 (b). **135 Alamy Stock Photo:** Artgen (bl). **Bridgeman Images:** © Fine Art Images (tl). **The Metropolitan Museum of Art:** Bequest of Alice K. Bache, 1977 (br); Gift and Bequest of Alice K. Bache, 1974, 1977 (tr); The Michael C. Rockefeller Memorial Collection, Purchase, Nelson A. Rockefeller Gift, 1967 (cb). **136 Alamy Stock Photo:** Album (cb). **Bridgeman Images:** © Bodleian Libraries, University of Oxford (b); © Boltin Picture Library (t). **Library of Congress, Washington, D.C.:** Bernardino De Sahagún (cl); Bernardino De Sahagún (cr). **137 Bridgeman Images:** © Bodleian Libraries, University of Oxford. **138-139 Alamy Stock Photo:** History_Docu_Photo. **140 Alamy Stock Photo:** Heritage Image Partnership Ltd / Werner Forman Archive / British Museum, London (br). **Getty Images:** Universal Images Group / Werner Forman (tc); Universal Images Group / Werner Forman (bc). **Shutterstock.com:** Gianni Dagli Orti (tr). **140-141 Library of Congress, Washington, D.C.:** Bernardino De Sahagún (c). **141 Alamy Stock Photo:** Zoltan Bagosi (tr); Penta Springs Limited / Artokoloro (bc); Historic Collection (br). **Library of Congress, Washington, D.C.:** Bernardino De Sahagún (cb). **143 Alamy Stock Photo:** Icom Images (br); The History Collection (cr). **Library of Congress, Washington, D.C.:** Bernardino De Sahagún (tr). **144-145 Alamy Stock Photo:** Art Collection. **146 Alamy Stock Photo:** GRANGER - Historical Picture Archive (c); Science History Images / Photo Researchers (t). **Getty Images:** De Agostini / De Agostini Picture Library (cr). **147 Alamy Stock Photo:** Piemags (tl); WHPics (b). **Library of Congress, Washington, D.C.:** Bernardino De Sahagún (tc). **148 Alamy Stock Photo:** GRANGER - Historical Picture Archive (cra); Science History Images / Photo Researchers (cla); WHPics (b). **149 Alamy Stock Photo:** Art Collection (tr); WHPics (tl); WHPics (b). **150 Alamy Stock Photo:** Geogphotos (bl); GRANGER - Historical Picture Archive (cr). **151 Alamy Stock Photo:** Blickwinkel / Hartl (cra); Frank Nowikowski / Banco de México Diego Rivera Frida Kahlo Museums Trust, Mexico, D.F. / © DACS 2025 (l). **Dorling Kindersley:** Tracy Morgan: S.Corrone; H.Hernandez; Terry; L.Woods (ca). **Dreamstime.com:** Svetlana Larina / Blair_witch (ca/Butterfly). **Getty Images / iStock:** Eve Orea (crb). **152 Alamy Stock Photo:** History and Art Collection (tc); Icom Images (tr). **Library of Congress, Washington, D.C.:** Bernardino De Sahagún (bc). **153 Alamy Stock Photo:** Leonardo Diaz Romero (r). **Getty Images:** De Agostini / Dea / G. Dagli Orti (cla); Universal Images Group / Werner Forman (bc)

Cover images: Front and Back: **Dreamstime.com:** Krystsina Birukova tc, Peter Hermes Furian (Frame 1), Macrovector cb; **Getty Images:** Marizol Mendez (Symbolism); **Shutterstock.com:** Panuwat Mamarksap (Frame 2); Front: **Dreamstime.com:** Maria Egupova br, Peter Hermes Furian cb, Peter Hermes Furian cb/ (Aztec god); Back: **Dreamstime.com:** Peter Hermes Furian bc, Peter Hermes Furian bc/ (Aztec god); Spine: **Dreamstime.com:** Peter Hermes Furian t, Peter Hermes Furian b; **Getty Images:** Marizol Mendez